Sis, Chill: Navigating Love with Confidence

Ember Blackwood

Published by Ali the narrator, 2023.

SIS, CHILL: NAVIGATING LOVE WITH CONFIDENCE

First edition. December 26, 2023.

ISBN: 979-8223525752

Written by Ember Blackwood.

Sis, Chill Navigating Love with Confidence

Sis, Chill: Navigating Love with Confidence

Published by: Ali the Narrator

ISBN:

anx·i·e·ty

æŋˈzaɪ.ɪ.ti

1. a minute tremor of unease, the indivisible essence of apprehension.
2. the wellspring of potent emotions, birthing waves of internal intensity.

Introduction

"Ever feel those predate jitters? Sis, chill! This book is your guide to conquering dating anxiety and transforming those nervous moments into opportunities for genuine connection."

In the wild world of dating, predate jitters are like the backstage nerves before a big show, shaping the whole romantic shebang. It's that heart-thumping moment when you're about to meet someone new, the mental gymnastics of figuring out what to say, and the worry that maybe your socks don't match your personality. But hold up, because dating anxiety isn't just a buzzkill; it's the secret sauce that flavors the whole dating experience. Picture this: excitement doing a cha-cha with self-doubt, and both of them grooving to the rhythm of potential connection. We're about to dive into the rollercoaster of emotions, from the thrill of a promising date to the sneaky shadows of "Am I good enough?" Exploring the impact of predate anxiety is like dissecting the heartbeat of vulnerability and resilience – a journey where nerves meet growth, self-discovery, and the chance for some seriously cool connections. So, grab your metaphorical popcorn, because this ride? It's about to get interesting!

Ever wondered why confidence is the secret sauce for whipping up successful and fulfilling relationships? Imagine this: You stride into a room, not with arrogance but with a quiet assurance, wearing your quirks like a badge of honor. Your uniqueness becomes a magnetic force, drawing people in like moths to a flame.

In the dating arena, confidence is your magic wand, turning a nerve-wracking date into a stage where you shine like the star you are. It's not about flawless perfection; it's about embracing your story, celebrating your journey, and radiating an energy that says, "I'm comfortable in my own skin."

As we embark on this adventure together, building confidence isn't just a checkmark on the dating to-do list; it's the golden key to unlocking the door to fulfilling relationships. Picture it as a superpower that guides you through the twists and turns of the dating landscape, from the initial heart-fluttering moments to the creation of deeper, more meaningful connections.

In these pages, we won't just talk about confidence; we'll breathe life into it, showing you how it transforms ordinary interactions into extraordinary experiences. It's not a one-size-fits-all formula but a journey of self-discovery and self-celebration. So, don that metaphorical confidence cape – we're about to embark on a journey where you become the author of your own love story, filled with successful and fulfilling connections.

Understanding Social Anxiety

Chapter 1

"Did you know? Social anxiety affects millions of people worldwide. But fear not, we're diving deep into what it really is and how it influences your dating life."

Social anxiety isn't just a trendy term; it's a mix of thoughts, feelings, and perspectives that can turn a seemingly simple coffee date into a bit of a high-stakes situation. In this chapter, we're not just scratching the surface; we're digging in to get to the core of social anxiety and understand how it plays a role in our dating adventures. So, grab your curiosity hat, because we're about to explore the ins and outs of social anxiety and how it shapes the way we navigate the world of connections.

Defining Social Anxiety in Dating

LET'S GET COZY AND chat about understanding the roots and manifestations of social anxiety in the dating game.

Imagine social anxiety as the shy cousin at the family reunion—it's there, but it might take a bit of digging to figure out why. The roots of social anxiety often weave into our past experiences, shaping how we perceive ourselves in social situations. Maybe it's that awkward dance at a school dance or a not-so-stellar moment during a group project. These little snippets from our past can grow into vines, influencing how we approach dating scenarios today.

Social anxiety is like a chameleon, taking on different forms for different people. For some, it's the racing heartbeat and sweaty palms before a date. For others, it might be the constant overthinking of every word and gesture, as if there's an invisible audience critiquing every move. Understanding these manifestations is like decoding the secret language of social anxiety. It's not always loud and clear; sometimes, it's a subtle whisper influencing our thoughts and actions.

So, here's the friendly advice: Take a moment to reflect on your own experiences. What moments from your past might be influencing how you approach dating now? And how does social anxiety show up for you? Understanding these roots and manifestations is like turning on a light in a previously dim room; it helps us see things more clearly and navigate the dating dance floor with a bit more ease.

Think of triggers as little landmines scattered across the dating landscape. They can be subtle, like the fear of not meeting someone's expectations, or a bit more pronounced, like the dread of being the center of attention. It's crucial to identify these triggers because, once you know where they are, you can navigate around them with a bit more finesse.

Common triggers often include the fear of judgment – that nagging worry about being scrutinized or not measuring up to some invisible standard. Then there's the pressure to conform to societal expectations, like feeling you have to be witty and charming at all times. It's like being handed an unspoken script and fearing you might forget your lines.

Take a moment to reflect on what sets off your social anxiety radar. Is it the fear of saying the wrong thing, or maybe the worry about being vulnerable? Recognizing these triggers is like having a treasure map to navigate the dating terrain. Once you know where the hidden challenges are, you can sidestep them with a bit more confidence. Remember, you're not alone in this – recognizing common triggers is a shared experience, and understanding them is a step toward reclaiming your dating confidence.

1. Fear of Judgment

- Worrying about being scrutinized or evaluated by your date.

- Feeling a constant pressure to meet perceived standards of attractiveness or social desirability.

- Second-guessing your actions and fearing negative judgment from others.

2. Pressure to Conform

- Feeling the need to conform to societal expectations of what a "good" date looks like.

- Struggling with the expectation to always be witty, charming, or effortlessly engaging.

- Fearing that deviating from conventional dating norms will lead to social rejection.

3. Concerns about Vulnerability

- Hesitating to share personal thoughts or experiences due to the fear of being judged.

- Feeling vulnerable when revealing aspects of your true self, such as insecurities or past challenges.

- Fearing that opening up may lead to rejection or negative perceptions.

4. Performance Anxiety

- Anxiety related to the perceived need to perform well during the date.

- Worrying about saying the wrong thing or making social blunders.

- Feeling as though the date is a performance where you must constantly impress.

Understanding and recognizing these common triggers is a significant step toward navigating social anxiety in the dating world. It allows for targeted strategies to address these specific challenges and paves the way for more authentic and relaxed interactions.

Let's delve into the world of nerves and social anxiety, where the line between the two isn't always crystal clear. Nervousness, that flutter of butterflies before a date, is like the starter pack for any social interaction. It's that normal, anticipatory jolt that makes things exciting. Now, social anxiety, on the other hand, is like the distant cousin who overstays their welcome. It's not just about the occasional jitters; it's an uninvited guest that lingers, coloring everyday interactions with a touch of unease. Picture nervousness as the fleeting joy of a rollercoaster ride, while social anxiety is more like the constant hum of stage fright, persisting even after the curtain falls. The distinction lies in the persistence and intensity; while nerves are momentary, social anxiety is a lingering presence, casting a shadow over the simplest of social exchanges. So, if you ever find yourself wondering whether it's just butterflies or something more, remember: the key lies in understanding the duration and impact, allowing you to navigate the dating dance with a clearer perspective. After all, everyone gets a little nervous, but when anxiety decides to stick around, it's time to take a closer look and approach things with a touch more compassion, both for yourself and others.

Let's illustrate the difference between nervousness and social anxiety with two relatable situations:

Nervousness:

Imagine you're waiting for your date at a cozy coffee shop. Your heart beats a little faster, and there's a delightful sense of anticipation. Your palms might be a touch sweaty, but it's the kind of nervous excitement that comes with any new experience. It's akin to the feeling before a thrilling rollercoaster ride—momentary, exhilarating, and soon to be replaced by the joy of the experience.

Social Anxiety:

Now, let's shift gears. You're at the same coffee shop, but this time, that initial excitement has morphed into a persistent unease. The thought of engaging in conversation makes your stomach tie itself into knots. You find yourself rehearsing potential scenarios in your mind, worrying about saying the wrong thing or being judged. Unlike the fleeting nerves, this social anxiety is like a constant companion, casting a shadow over the otherwise charming setting.

In these examples, nervousness is the brief, normal prelude to a new experience, while social anxiety lingers, impacting the way you engage with others. Recognizing these distinctions helps in understanding the nuances between everyday nerves and the more persistent presence of social anxiety in the dating realm.

Imagine you're on a date, and the normal, fleeting nerves begin to morph into something more persistent—social anxiety. It's like trying to blend oil and water; they just don't quite mix. While nervousness is a natural part of the dating experience, social anxiety, when left unacknowledged, can become a tricky companion, affecting the quality of your interactions.

The danger lies in misinterpreting the signals. If you chalk up the persistent unease to mere nerves, you might miss the opportunity to address deeper issues. Social anxiety, unlike the passing jitters, can impact self-esteem, hinder authentic expression, and even lead to avoidance of social situations altogether. It's like letting a small leak go unchecked; over time, it can turn into a more significant issue.

Mixing the two can also create a confusing cocktail of emotions. You might find yourself wondering why the initial excitement of a date transforms into an ongoing challenge. It's like trying to enjoy a beautiful day with a persistent rain cloud overhead. Recognizing the difference between nerves and social anxiety is crucial for setting realistic expectations, understanding your own emotional landscape, and fostering genuine connections.

So, the key is awareness. If those initial butterflies begin to feel more like a constant swarm, it's worth taking a moment to reflect. Acknowledge the difference between the normal ebb and flow of nerves and the persistent presence of social anxiety. By doing so, you can navigate the dating landscape with a clearer understanding of yourself and, ultimately, cultivate more meaningful connections.

The Impact on Self-Perception

EVER HAD THOSE MOMENTS where your internal dialogue takes center stage, whispering doubts and fueling insecurities? Welcome to the theater of self-esteem, a crucial player in the world of social anxiety. Social anxiety often casts a shadow on how we view ourselves, influencing the narrative of our own worth and desirability.

Think of self-esteem as the foundation of a house. When it's sturdy, you stand tall and confident. However, social anxiety can be like termites, quietly gnawing at that foundation. It's not about external validation; it's about how you perceive your own value in the grand play of social interactions.

Low self-esteem becomes a fertile ground for social anxiety to take root. Thoughts like "I'm not interesting enough" or "I'll mess up and embarrass myself" become the unwelcome chorus. These thoughts aren't reflective of reality but are distorted reflections in the funhouse mirrors of anxiety.

So, here's the real talk: social anxiety has a knack for convincing you that you're not enough. But in the dating game, understanding the role of self-esteem is your secret weapon. It's not about transforming into someone you're not; it's about embracing your authentic self.

Ever notice how social anxiety can be a bit like wearing glasses with the wrong prescription? It skews the way you see yourself, and dating confidence takes the hit. Distorted self-perception becomes the ghostwriter of your dating script, penning narratives that might not align with the truth.

Imagine going on a date with a funhouse mirror in your mind. The distortion might make you see flaws that others wouldn't even notice. Thoughts like "I'm not attractive enough" or "I'll say something stupid" become the background music, drowning out the potential for genuine connection.

Distorted self-perception doesn't just whisper doubts; it shouts them from the rooftops. It's like carrying around an invisible backpack filled with insecurities, making each step on the dating path feel heavier than it should. The danger here is that these distorted perceptions can become self-fulfilling prophecies, influencing your behavior and potentially affecting the outcome of the date.

Dating confidence isn't about perfection; it's about embracing your imperfect, wonderfully unique self. Social anxiety might try to hijack the script, but understanding how distorted self-perception plays a role is your secret weapon.

Ready to flip the script and embrace a version of yourself that radiates confidence? Say goodbye to self-doubt and hello to a positive self-image. We're about to unpack some game-changing strategies that will have you strutting through the dating scene with a newfound sense of self-assured charm.

1. Embrace Your Uniqueness

- Celebrate the quirks and idiosyncrasies that make you, well, you.

- Recognize that perfection is a myth, and it's the imperfections that add character.

2. Challenge Negative Thoughts

- Identify and challenge distorted thoughts that undermine your self-worth.

- Replace negative self-talk with positive affirmations and realistic perspectives.

3. Focus on Strengths and Achievements

- Acknowledge your accomplishments, both big and small.

- Identify your strengths and allow them to take center stage in your self-perception.

4. Practice Self-Compassion

- Treat yourself with the same kindness and understanding you'd offer a friend.

- Accept that everyone makes mistakes, and they don't define your worth.

5. Surround Yourself with Positivity

- Build a supportive network of friends who uplift and encourage you.

- Limit exposure to negative influences and cultivate an environment that fosters positivity.

6. Set Realistic Goals

- Break down larger goals into manageable, achievable steps.

- Celebrate progress, and don't let setbacks derail your positive self-image.

7. Engage in Self-Care

- Prioritize activities that bring joy and relaxation.

- Nurture your physical and mental well-being, as they are interconnected with self-image.

8. Seek Professional Support

- Consider therapy or counseling to explore and address underlying issues.

- Professionals can provide tools and guidance for building a positive self-image.

Cultivating a positive self-image is an ongoing journey, and these strategies are your roadmap to confidently embrace the unique and wonderful individual that you are. Get ready to rewrite the narrative and step into a version of yourself that radiates authenticity and self-love.

Breaking the Stigma

SOCIAL ANXIETY OFTEN comes with its fair share of myths, like unwelcome baggage it carries along. One common misconception is that it's just shyness taken up a notch. Picture this: shyness is like a gentle breeze, while social anxiety can feel more like a whirlwind of worry and self-doubt. Addressing these misconceptions is essential to understanding the unique challenges that social anxiety presents.

Another myth is that individuals with social anxiety are just being overly sensitive or seeking attention. It's crucial to recognize that social anxiety isn't a choice or a desire for the spotlight; it's an internal struggle that can impact various aspects of a person's life, especially when it comes to navigating the intricacies of dating.

By setting the record straight on these misconceptions, we pave the way for empathy and understanding. Social anxiety is not a mere preference for solitude, nor is it a bid for sympathy. It's a genuine, often overwhelming challenge that deserves acknowledgment and support.

So, let's break free from these myths and open up a space for authentic conversations. By understanding the realities of social anxiety, we can foster a dating landscape that embraces diversity in experiences, making room for connections that go beyond the surface. It's time to challenge those misconceptions and create a more inclusive and compassionate dating environment for everyone.

1. **Misconception: Social Anxiety is Just Extreme Shyness**

- **Reality**: While shyness involves a mild discomfort in social situations, social anxiety goes beyond, causing intense fear and anxiety that can significantly impact daily life.

- **Why it Matters**: Recognizing the distinction is crucial for understanding the depth of challenges individuals with social anxiety face and providing appropriate support.

1. **Misconception: People with Social Anxiety Just Want Attention**

- **Reality**: Social anxiety is not a bid for attention; it's an internal struggle characterized by a fear of judgment and negative evaluation in social situations.

- **Why it Matters**: Dispelling this myth helps shift the narrative, fostering empathy and encouraging open communication about the real challenges of social anxiety.

1. **Misconception: Social Anxiety is a Choice or a Form of Laziness**

- **Reality**: Social anxiety is not a conscious decision or a lack of effort; it's a mental health condition rooted in complex factors like genetics, brain chemistry, and life experiences.

- **Why it Matters**: Understanding that social anxiety is not a matter of choice reduces stigma, allowing for more compassionate and supportive interactions.

In a society where whispers often drown out the conversations about mental health, it's time to turn up the volume and open the dialogue surrounding social anxiety. Picture these conversations as doors leading to understanding, empathy, and connection. By breaking the silence, we can clarify misconceptions about social anxiety, creating a more informed and supportive community. Open discussions also play a pivotal role in destigmatizing mental health, challenging preconceived notions and fostering acceptance.

As we swing these doors wide, a ripple effect of empathy is set into motion. Individuals sharing their personal experiences with social anxiety not only provide insight into the challenges they face but also foster empathy among peers. These open conversations highlight common ground, emphasizing that struggles with mental health are more widespread than one might think, creating a sense of shared experience and solidarity.

Moreover, encouraging open discussions about mental health helps build supportive environments where individuals feel comfortable seeking help and sharing their journeys. Social anxiety can be isolating, but these conversations break down barriers, reminding individuals that they are not alone in their experiences. By fostering these supportive networks, we reduce the stigma associated with seeking help, creating spaces where individuals can find encouragement and understanding.

Open conversations also serve as powerful tools for education and empowerment. They contribute to broader mental health awareness, dispelling myths and providing accurate information about conditions like social anxiety. By increasing awareness, we empower individuals to recognize when they need support and to seek professional help without fear of judgment.

In a world where mental health conversations are often hushed, promoting open discussions about social anxiety not only breaks down barriers but also creates a culture where understanding, compassion, and support thrive. It's time to amplify these conversations, making mental health discussions as common as talking about the weather, and fostering a world where everyone's experiences are acknowledged and valued.

Okay, imagine our emotions as this big, colorful quilt we're all sewing together. Now, social anxiety? It's like a thread we're weaving into the fabric. So, let's talk about making that thread feel right at home, not like an outsider.

First off, let's celebrate that social anxiety isn't a one-size-fits-all thing. It's more like a bunch of unique stories. Each person's experience is like a different color in our emotional quilt—valid, real, and totally okay.

Think of social anxiety as a unique skill, not a weakness. It's the part of you that shows you're brave enough to face challenges. See, it's not a flaw; it's your superhero cape in the world of social interactions.

Encouraging folks to share their stories isn't just breaking the ice; it's melting the entire iceberg. We're saying no to fancy jargon and yes to real, honest conversations. It's like taking off the superhero mask and letting everyone see the real you.

Creating spaces where judgment fears to tread? That's the vibe. It's like turning a room full of strangers into a cozy gathering of friends. In these friendly communities, everyone's quirks are celebrated. It's not about fitting into a mold; it's about embracing the beautiful mess of being human.

And education? Think of it as the flashlight guiding us through the dark corners. It's spreading the word, letting everyone know that social anxiety isn't a rare bird; it's just another feather in our emotional cap.

So, our mission is clear: let's not hide the thread of social anxiety; let's flaunt it. In a world where everyone's stitching their unique patch into the quilt, we're making sure social anxiety gets its moment in the spotlight. It's about turning shame into acceptance and understanding, making our emotional quilt the coziest, most inclusive one around.

The Power of Vulnerability

THE KIND THAT'S LIKE laying your cards on the table. Imagine dating as this unpredictable dance, and vulnerability? It's the spontaneous spin that adds a bit of thrill.

Dating, we know, is a bit of an emotional rollercoaster. Now, vulnerability is like strapping in and saying, "Here I am, no frills or fancy filters." It's not about being perfect; it's about being genuine, quirks and all.

Sure, vulnerability can be a bit scary. What if they don't like the real you? What if it doesn't work out? Those are legit worries, but here's the thing: vulnerability isn't about being fearless; it's about being courageous despite the fear.

Here's the magic trick—vulnerability turns a date from "just fine" to "there's something special here." It's like opening a window and letting someone see the real view, not just the carefully curated Instagram version.

Worried about being judged? Totally get it! But vulnerability isn't about pouring your heart out to everyone. It's about finding someone who appreciates your quirks and thinks, "Yep, this is my kind of wonderful."

Think of vulnerability as the bridge to deeper connections. It's that handshake turning into a hug, that unspoken "I've got your back" agreement. When you bring your real self into the mix, it builds this trust bridge that turns dating into something more profound.

And here's the cool part—when both sides bring their vulnerability game, it's like a duet. Shared vulnerability makes connections stronger. It's admitting, "I've got insecurities too," and finding solace in the fact that neither of you has it all figured out.

So, in the dance of dating, let vulnerability be your signature move. It's not a sign of weakness; it's a badge of courage. Embrace the uncertainty, show your true colors, and watch how vulnerability transforms the dating game into something authentic, unfiltered, and beautifully real.

Let's talk about the real glue that binds connections—sharing vulnerabilities. It's like opening up a treasure chest and letting someone peek inside, flaws and all.

Breaking Down Walls:

When you share your vulnerabilities, it's like chipping away at those walls we all build. It's an invitation that says, "Hey, I trust you with the unfiltered me." That kind of trust is the foundation of something real.

Creating a Safe Space:

Sharing vulnerabilities creates this safe haven. It's saying, "Here are the things I might not show everyone, but I'll show you." It's a space where judgment takes a backseat, and understanding takes the wheel.

Deepening Understanding:

Think of it as turning the volume up on understanding. When you let someone see your vulnerabilities, it's like saying, "This is what makes me tick, and I want you to know." It's an invitation to understand the layers beneath the surface.

Building Empathy:

Empathy is the magic that happens when you realize someone else's struggles aren't that different from yours. Sharing vulnerabilities is like giving each other a roadmap to empathy. It's the "I get it, I've been there" connection that fosters a deeper bond.

Strength in Vulnerability:

There's a paradoxical strength in vulnerability. It's not about being weak; it's about being brave enough to say, "This is me, take it or leave it." It's that rare authenticity that sparks a genuine connection.

Mutual Vulnerability:

Now, here's where the magic intensifies—when both sides bring their vulnerabilities to the table. It's not a competition; it's a partnership. It's saying, "I'll show you mine if you show me yours." This mutual sharing creates a unique dance of understanding and acceptance.

So, in the grand scheme of connections, sharing vulnerabilities isn't a risk; it's an investment. It's an investment in authenticity, understanding, and a connection that goes beyond the surface. When you open up about your vulnerabilities, you're not just sharing your story; you're creating a space for someone else to share theirs, fostering a connection that's as real as it gets.

Let's tackle the big, intimidating monster in the room—fear of judgment. It's that sneaky voice that whispers, "What if they don't like the real you?" Well, let's turn up the volume on a counter-narrative that says, "What if they do?"

Reality Check:

First things first, everyone feels the jitters about being judged. It's like a universal part of the human experience, sort of like getting nervous before a big exam. But here's the thing: those judgments are often more about the judger than the judged.

Vulnerability as a Shield:

Now, imagine vulnerability as this superhero shield. When you show your true self, quirks and all, it's like putting on that shield and saying,

"I'm invincible because I'm being real." It's not about being bulletproof; it's about being authentic.

Selective Audiences:

Guess what? Not everyone deserves a front-row seat to your vulnerability show. It's more like a VIP invitation-only event. The ones who truly matter won't judge; they'll appreciate the courage it takes to be authentic.

Reframing Judgment:

Let's reframe judgment as a filter, not a brick wall. When someone judges, it's like a filter saying, "This might not be your people." It's not a rejection; it's a redirection to those who genuinely get you.

Dropping the Perfection Act:

The fear of judgment often stems from trying to be perfect. But, let's be real—perfection is overrated. Embrace the messy, imperfect, wonderfully flawed you. It's the most genuine version, and that's what creates real connections.

Self-Compassion Toolkit:

Equip yourself with a self-compassion toolkit. It's filled with reminders that you're human, you're doing your best, and you're allowed to be imperfect. When the fear of judgment creeps in, open that toolkit and remind yourself that vulnerability is strength, not weakness.

Celebrating Uniqueness:

Lastly, let's celebrate uniqueness. The things that make you different are your superpowers. Instead of fearing judgment, let's own those quirks and wear them like a badge of honor. Authenticity attracts authenticity, after all.

So, when the fear of judgment knocks on your door, don't be afraid to answer. Show it your vulnerability superhero shield, introduce it to your self-compassion toolkit, and let it know you're on a journey of embracing the wonderfully imperfect you. The fear of judgment? It might not vanish entirely, but with the right mindset, it certainly loses its power.

Mind-Body Connection

IMAGINE YOUR BODY AND mind as dance partners in a lively tango. Each step they take influences the other, creating a unique rhythm that shapes your overall well-being. Have you ever noticed how tension in your shoulders can mimic the stress in your thoughts, or how a deep breath can be the perfect move to a more relaxed state?

It's like they're part of a dynamic duo, responding to each other's cues on the dance floor of your existence. This connection is not just about the physical and mental doing their own thing; it's a collaborative dance, an intricate conversation that impacts how you feel and move through life.

Now, let's flip the record and talk about mindfulness – think of it as the DJ playing the right tunes for this dance. Being mindful is like setting the stage for a smoother, more harmonious interaction between body and mind. It's the art of paying attention to the present moment, guiding this dance away from the chaotic shuffle of social anxiety.

And get this – we have some nifty practices to keep you grounded, like having the perfect dance partner to navigate the twists and turns of the anxiety waltz. So, get ready to waltz into the captivating connection between your physical and mental states, where every move counts and every breath shapes the dance of your well-being!

Alright, let's embark on a journey into the realm of mindfulness, a powerful ally in the quest to ease the grip of social anxiety.

Imagine mindfulness as your trusted companion, a steady guide through the maze of anxious thoughts. It's not a magical fix, but more like a flashlight in the darkness, helping you navigate the twists and turns of social interactions with a bit more ease.

Think of it as a subtle shift in focus, a mental pivot from the worries of the future or past to the richness of the present moment. Mindfulness is like an anchor, grounding you amidst the storm of anxious thoughts that often accompany social situations.

Now, let's get practical. Picture this: you're in the midst of a social gathering, heart rate picking up, mind buzzing with "what ifs." This is where mindfulness steps in, offering a simple yet profound tool – your breath. Taking a moment to focus on each inhale and exhale becomes a mini sanctuary, a brief respite from the whirlwind of anxiety.

It's not about erasing the discomfort; it's about acknowledging it and, in that acknowledgment, finding a moment of calm. Mindfulness is that pause button, allowing you to respond thoughtfully rather than react impulsively to the challenges of social anxiety.

So, as you navigate the landscape of social interactions, let mindfulness be your gentle guide. It's not a quick-fix remedy, but rather a skill you cultivate, a muscle you strengthen over time. And in this cultivation, you discover a tool that, with consistent practice, becomes a reliable companion on the journey to alleviating the weight of social anxiety.

Practices for staying present and grounded:

- **Mindful Breathing:**

○ Anchor to your breath, using it as a constant presence in the present moment.

○ When distractions arise, gently redirect your focus to the sensation of breathing.

○ Practice diaphragmatic breathing for a deeper and more grounding experience.

○ Incorporate short breathing exercises throughout the day to maintain mindfulness.

- **Cultivating Mindful Awareness:**

○ Develop a non-judgmental awareness of your thoughts and emotions.

○ Observe them without attachment, acknowledging their presence without getting entangled.

○ Consider mindfulness meditation to enhance your ability to stay present.

○ Integrate mindfulness into daily activities, such as eating or walking, to foster continuous awareness.

- **Engaging the Senses:**

○ Bring attention to your surroundings, noticing textures, scents, and sounds.

○ Practice mindful eating by savoring each bite and paying attention to flavors.

○ Explore a mindful listening exercise, focusing on one specific sound in your environment.

○ Ground yourself in the present by physically connecting with objects—feeling their weight or texture.

As we wrap up this chapter, we've taken a deep dive into the world of social anxiety in dating. From understanding its roots to recognizing triggers, we've faced the challenges and celebrated transformative moments. By breaking down misconceptions and fostering open conversations, we've made strides in normalizing the social anxiety experience, creating a more compassionate space. Embracing vulnerability has been our secret weapon, turning awkward moments into genuine connections and conquering the fear of judgment. Exploring the mind-body connection, we've added a touch of mindfulness to ease social anxiety, adopting friendly strategies for staying present and grounded. Remember, this journey is all about self-discovery and transforming those predate jitters into the confidence that fuels genuine connections. Onward to the next chapter!

Choosing Comfortable Environments

Chapter 2

"Ready to redefine your dating narrative? Explore the transformative impact of selecting comfortable environments, where the ambiance sets the stage for genuine connections to bloom."

Identifying Ideal Date Locations

IN THE FASCINATING world of crafting the perfect date, there's a profound truth we're about to unveil—the power of personal preferences in shaping an unforgettable experience. Think of it like tailoring a suit; each detail contributes to the comfort and style of the overall look. So, here's our first insight: considering personal preferences is the secret sauce that can turn a date into a truly authentic and enjoyable adventure.

Picture this: a date uniquely curated to align with individual tastes, from the ambiance to the activities. It's about creating an environment where every moment feels like a bespoke experience, a reflection of your desires and passions. This personalized touch is where the magic happens, fostering a connection that goes beyond the ordinary.

Now, let's turn our attention to a subtle yet mighty force in the realm of dating—the influence of ambiance on mood. Picture the ambiance as the painter's brush, adding hues and tones to the canvas of your date. It's not just about the physical surroundings; it's the emotional undertones that set the stage for a remarkable experience.

Consider this: the warm glow of soft lighting in a cozy corner, or the vibrant energy of a bustling cafe. These are more than mere settings; they're ingredients in the recipe for a mood that can sway the entire vibe of your date. We're about to dive into the nuances of how ambiance becomes the silent conductor, orchestrating the emotional symphony of your rendezvous.

Let's delve into two distinct setups to showcase how ambiance can be the subtle architect of mood:

Setup 1: Cozy Corner Café

Imagine a quaint corner in a charming café, bathed in the warm glow of soft, ambient lighting. The gentle hum of conversations creates an intimate atmosphere. The aroma of freshly ground coffee beans wafts through the air, creating a sense of comfort. Soft jazz tunes play in the background, contributing to a relaxed and cozy vibe. The small, intimate tables encourage closeness, fostering a feeling of connection. This setup is perfect for those seeking a more laid-back, romantic ambiance, where the focus is on quiet conversations and shared moments.

Setup 2: Trendy Rooftop Bar

Now, shift the scene to a trendy rooftop bar with panoramic city views. The ambiance here is dynamic and vibrant, with upbeat music and the lively chatter of fellow patrons. The sleek, modern décor and neon accents add an element of excitement. The open space and expansive views create an exhilarating atmosphere. This setup is ideal for those looking to infuse energy and a sense of adventure into their date, where the mood is dynamic, and the setting encourages a more lively and spirited interaction.

In these setups, the ambiance becomes a silent storyteller, shaping the mood in unique ways. It's not just about where you are; it's about how the setting orchestrates the emotional undertones, creating a distinct mood for your date.

THERE EXISTS A HIDDEN realm of unconventional yet cozy venues—an enchanting exploration that transcends the ordinary and infuses a sense of adventure into the traditional rendezvous. Picture this: an intimate speakeasy tucked behind a bookshelf, where the hushed ambiance and vintage decor create an air of mystery. Or perhaps a botanical garden transformed into a twinkling wonderland at night, where paths lined with fairy lights beckon to wanderers seeking a touch of magic.

These unconventional venues are not just spaces; they're experiences waiting to unfold. Imagine stepping into an art gallery after hours, where the soft glow of spotlights transforms paintings into portals of inspiration. The hum of creativity and the scent of fresh paint become accomplices in crafting an ambiance that sparks both dialogue and imagination.

The beauty of exploring these offbeat venues lies in the shared discovery, the sense of venturing into uncharted territory together. It's about breaking free from the predictable dinner-and-movie routine, embracing the unexpected, and letting the surroundings become active participants in the date.

Consider an evening spent in a retro arcade, where the nostalgic bleeps and bloops of vintage games become a soundtrack to laughter and playful banter. These venues breathe life into dates, offering an opportunity to connect on a deeper level by experiencing something genuinely novel.

Where every step holds the potential for magic, exploring unconventional yet cozy venues is an invitation to create memories that transcend the ordinary. It's about finding hidden corners that resonate with the uniqueness of your connection, turning a simple date into an adventure where surprises lurk around every corner. So, dare to step off the beaten path, and let the journey into these unconventional havens become a tale to be shared and cherished.

Rooftop Camping Retreat:

Elevate the traditional camping experience by setting up a cozy rooftop retreat. Pitch a tent, scatter cushions and blankets, and create a comfortable outdoor haven on your rooftop. Enjoy the intimacy of camping under the stars while still having the comforts of home close by. As you share stories, gaze at the night sky, and bask in the city lights below, this unconventional venue transforms your rooftop into a unique camping escape right in the heart of your urban landscape.

Pros:

- **Intimate Setting:** Offers a private and intimate camping experience, elevated above the hustle and bustle of the city.
- **Urban Escape:** Provides a unique opportunity to enjoy the outdoors and stargazing while still being in the comfort of your own home.
- **City Lights View:** Immerse yourself in the beauty of city lights below, adding a romantic ambiance to your camping adventure.

Cons:

- **Weather Dependency:** Vulnerable to weather conditions; rain or extreme temperatures might impact the experience.
- **Space Limitations:** Limited space compared to traditional camping sites, making it suitable for cozy, smaller gatherings.
- **Accessibility:** Requires a suitable rooftop space, limiting its feasibility for everyone.

Lakeside Bonfire Lounge:

Bring the charm of a lakeside retreat to your own backyard with a lakeside bonfire lounge. Set up a fire pit surrounded by comfortable seating, and enjoy the warmth of a crackling fire. Add a touch of romance with fairy lights strung around, creating a lakeside ambiance. As you unwind by the fire, share tales, roast marshmallows, and savor the serenity of a lakeside escape without leaving home. This unconventional venue offers the perfect blend of relaxation and intimacy, turning your backyard into a lakeside haven.

Pros:

- **Cozy Atmosphere:** Creates a cozy and romantic atmosphere with the warmth of a crackling bonfire.

- **Backyard Escape:** Transforms your backyard into a lakeside retreat, offering a serene and relaxing setting.

- **Easy Set-Up:** Relatively easy to set up with a fire pit and comfortable seating.

- **Cons:**

- **Fire Regulations:** Depending on local regulations, there might be restrictions on open fires, impacting the feasibility.

- **Weather Sensitivity:** Weather conditions can affect the comfort, with rain or wind potentially disrupting the bonfire experience.

- **Space Requirements:** Requires a spacious backyard to accommodate the fire pit and seating comfortably.

Vintage Picnic Tram Ride:

Infuse a touch of nostalgia into your date by exploring your city on a vintage tram turned into a picnic venue. Many cities offer vintage tram rides with refurbished interiors, creating a unique and cozy setting.

Pack a picnic basket with your favorite treats, hop aboard the tram, and enjoy a leisurely ride through the city streets. The rhythmic sway of the tram, coupled with the vintage charm, sets the stage for a delightful and unconventional picnic experience. This venue combines the romance of a bygone era with the joy of discovery, making it a memorable date option.

Pros:

- **Nostalgic Charm:** Infuses a sense of nostalgia and romance, creating a unique and memorable atmosphere.
- **City Exploration:** Allows for a leisurely exploration of the city while enjoying a vintage tram ride.
- **Relaxed Setting:** Provides a relaxed and charming setting for a picnic, combining transportation and dining.

Cons:

- **Availability:** Limited to cities that offer vintage tram rides, restricting accessibility.
- **Scheduling Challenges:** Requires coordination with tram schedules, potentially limiting flexibility.
- **Potential Crowds:** Popular vintage tram rides may attract crowds, impacting the privacy of the picnic experience.

Discovering your ideal date locations isn't just about finding picturesque spots but creating moments that resonate with comfort and connection. By considering personal preferences and exploring unconventional venues, you're not just picking places; you're crafting the backdrop for shared experiences that turn ordinary dates into extraordinary memories. So, let the journey to your ideal date locations be a delightful exploration, weaving the tapestry of your unique connection.

Nature as a Calming Element

NATURE EMERGES AS A calming thread, weaving a tranquil backdrop for your date. The therapeutic power of nature isn't a mere setting but a gentle guide, inviting you to immerse yourselves in its calming embrace.

As you step into the outdoors, feel the stress of the everyday hustle dissipate amidst the rustling leaves and the soft whispers of the wind. Nature becomes a sanctuary, offering a respite from the chaos and grounding you in the serenity of the present moment.

The therapeutic influence of nature goes beyond aesthetics; it shapes the atmosphere for shared activities. Whether it's a leisurely stroll through a verdant park, a lakeside picnic with the gentle lapping of water, or an adventurous hike through scenic trails, nature becomes the canvas on which your connection unfolds.

So, envision a date where nature isn't just a passive observer; it's an active participant, infusing tranquility into your shared experience. Together, you'll discover the calming elements of nature, turning your date into a harmonious blend of relaxation and genuine connection.

Park Bench Chill:

Keep it simple and intimate by finding a cozy park bench. Enjoy each other's company, bask in the fresh air, and watch the world go by. Bring along a light snack or coffee to enhance the laid-back atmosphere.

Pros:

- **Intimacy:** The simplicity of a park bench creates an intimate setting for one-on-one conversation.
- **Observation:** Watching the world go by offers interesting people-watching opportunities.
- **Casual:** Requires minimal planning and allows for a spontaneous connection.

Cons:

- **Weather Dependent:** Outdoor seating is subject to weather conditions.
- **Limited Comfort:** Park benches may not be as comfortable for extended periods.

Sunset Blanket Lounge:

Grab a comfortable blanket and head to a scenic spot to catch the sunset. Lounge together, share stories, and appreciate the changing hues of the sky as the day transitions to night. It's a serene way to connect in a relaxed outdoor setting.

Pros:

- **Romantic Atmosphere:** Sunset viewing provides a naturally romantic backdrop.
- **Comfort:** A blanket adds coziness, making it an ideal setting for relaxation.
- **Aesthetic Pleasure:** Appreciating the changing sky colors enhances the experience.

Cons:

- **Time Sensitivity:** Dependent on the sunset time, which may vary.

- **Weather Dependency:** Outdoor conditions can impact the comfort of the experience.

Nature Walk and Talk:

Opt for a leisurely nature walk in a nearby park or nature reserve. The unhurried pace allows for easy conversation while enjoying the beauty of the outdoors. Choose a trail with scenic views or interesting flora to add a touch of exploration to your date.

Pros:

- **Connection**: Walking side by side encourages a natural and easy flow of conversation.

- **Scenic Beauty:** Enjoying nature's beauty enhances the overall experience.

- **Health Benefits:** Combines outdoor activity with quality time.

Cons:

- **Physical Activity:** Not suitable for everyone, especially those with mobility issues.

- **Time Consuming:** Requires a longer time commitment than stationary activities.

Riverside Reflections:

Seek out a tranquil riverside location and let the calming sounds of flowing water set the backdrop for your date. Bring a blanket or find a comfortable spot by the riverbank to unwind, chat, and appreciate the serenity of the surroundings.

Pros:

- **Tranquility:** The calming sounds of flowing water create a peaceful atmosphere.
- **Scenic Setting:** Riverside locations often offer picturesque views.
- **Versatility:** Suitable for both daytime and evening settings.

Cons:

- **Accessibility:** Finding the right riverside spot may require some exploration.
- **Seasonal Considerations:** Weather and water levels can impact the experience.

Each outdoor date option has its unique charm, and the pros and cons provide a guide for choosing the one that best aligns with personal preferences and circumstances.

Alright, picture this romantic scenario – you and your partner paddling together in a kayak on a serene lakeside. The rhythmic dip of the paddles becomes a sort of synchronized dance, and the laughter shared echoes the harmony of your connection. But hold on, the magic doesn't stop there.

Imagine a peaceful forest hike where sunlight filters through leaves, casting a soft glow on the trail. You and your partner walk hand in hand, surrounded by the soothing scents of pine and the satisfying crunch of leaves underfoot. It's not just a walk; it's a shared journey that deepens your connection with each other and with nature.

Now, if you're up for some playful fun, how about a nature-inspired scavenger hunt? Amongst the trees and hidden spots, embark on a quest to find treasures – both natural and unexpected. The thrill of discovery becomes a shared victory, turning a simple walk into an adventure filled with laughter and a bit of friendly competition.

Nature's embrace also provides space for quieter moments. Picture a secluded beach at twilight, where you and your partner sit side by side, engrossed in the meditative art of building sandcastles. Each grain of sand becomes a part of a memory you're creating together – simple, profound, and uniquely yours.

These shared activities in nature go beyond the ordinary, creating a cozy haven for your relationship to blossom. Whether you're feeling the rush of an outdoor adventure or savoring the tranquility of a shared sunset, the tapestry woven from these moments becomes a testament to the richness of your connection – a masterpiece painted with the brushstrokes of love, laughter, and the beauty of the natural world.

The Role of Familiarity

NAVIGATING THE WORLD of dating can sometimes feel like stepping into uncharted territory. But fear not, because familiarity is your trusty compass in this journey. Leveraging familiarity isn't about sticking to the same old routine; it's about weaving the comfort of the known into the excitement of the new.

Think of it as meeting at your favorite local coffee shop or choosing a familiar park for a leisurely stroll. The comforting ambiance becomes a backdrop for connection, providing a sense of ease in the midst of the unknown. It's like meeting an old friend in a new setting – the familiarity acts as a friendly face in the crowd of uncertainties.

Leveraging familiarity is about creating a space where both you and your date feel at home. It's that cozy nook in the neighborhood that holds shared memories or the charming street where you first discovered your favorite gelato spot. By choosing familiar settings, you're not just relying on the known; you're transforming those spaces into chapters of your evolving story.

So, whether it's the corner booth at your regular diner or the park bench where you've shared countless laughs, familiarity becomes the anchor in the unpredictable sea of dating. It's your secret weapon against predate jitters, offering a comforting embrace that says, "You're not alone; you're with someone who knows the comfort of the familiar as much as you do." In this dance of old and new, familiarity becomes the reassuring partner, allowing you to twirl through the steps of connection with confidence and ease.

What if your favorite hangout spots could become the stage for a new chapter in your dating story? Incorporating your cherished haunts into your dates isn't just about revisiting the familiar; it's about transforming those spots into the backdrop of shared experiences and new adventures.

Consider that quirky bookstore where you've spent hours lost in the pages of novels – now, it becomes the perfect spot for a literary-themed date. You and your partner can explore new reads together, exchanging thoughts and recommendations, turning a familiar space into a canvas for shared interests.

Or how about that charming local art gallery where you've marveled at countless exhibitions? Turn it into a date night filled with conversations about art, perspectives, and the emotions that each piece evokes. The familiar walls of the gallery become witnesses to the blossoming connection between you and your date.

Incorporating favorite hangouts into dates is like putting a fresh spin on a classic song. It's the melody of familiarity with a new arrangement of experiences. That cozy pub where you've celebrated victories and weathered storms can become the backdrop for a laid-back evening of laughter, reminiscing, and creating new memories.

These familiar haunts aren't just locations; they're the settings where your stories unfold. By bringing your favorite hangouts into your dates, you're inviting your partner into the narrative of your life. It's a shared journey through spaces that hold meaning for you, turning every corner and table into a potential scene for connection and romance. So, let your favorite hangouts play a starring role in your dating escapades, because in the familiarity, you're not just revisiting places; you're crafting a love story uniquely yours.

Creating a sense of comfort through shared experiences is like weaving a cozy blanket of connection, one thread at a time. It's not just about the activities; it's about the laughter, the moments of vulnerability, and the joy that comes from building a shared history.

Imagine cooking together in the kitchen, the aroma of a favorite dish filling the air. It's not just a meal; it's a collaborative creation, a shared experience that turns an ordinary evening into a delightful journey of tastes and stories. The familiarity of the kitchen becomes the canvas for a masterpiece made with love.

Taking a weekend getaway to a familiar spot is another way to cultivate comfort through shared experiences. Whether it's a cabin in the woods or a beachside retreat, the environment becomes a cocoon for connection. Every wave, every rustle of leaves, becomes a shared symphony, fostering an intimate bond in the serenity of the familiar.

Shared experiences also unfold in the simple moments, like binge-watching a favorite TV series or playing board games on a rainy afternoon. These seemingly ordinary activities become the threads that stitch together the fabric of your relationship. The comfort of shared routines and rituals builds a foundation of trust and understanding.

Moreover, facing challenges together creates a unique sense of comfort. Overcoming obstacles, big or small, strengthens the connection and reinforces the idea that you're a team. It's the shared triumphs and the joint problem-solving that shape the narrative of your relationship, adding depth and resilience to your bond.

In essence, creating a sense of comfort through shared experiences is about more than the activities themselves; it's about the shared narratives, the mutual growth, and the comfort found in knowing that you're creating a life together, one shared experience at a time.

Personalizing the Experience

HAVE YOU EVER FOUND yourself stuck in the cycle of repetitive and uninspiring dates, wondering how to inject a spark of uniqueness into your romantic adventures? Fear not! The answer lies in the transformative power of personalization. In this extensive guide, we'll delve into the art of tailoring dates to individual interests, crafting experiences that feel authentic, and exploring the profound impact of personalization on connection. Get ready to embark on a journey of discovery, creating memories that are as unique as you are.

Your interests are the building blocks of your personality, and integrating them into your dates adds a layer of authenticity that resonates deeply. Let's explore how to tailor dates to individual interests, making each experience a celebration of your unique tastes.

Knowing Your Passions:

Understanding what truly sparks your enthusiasm is the first step toward creating personalized and memorable dates. Reflect on your hobbies, interests, and the activities that bring you joy.

Diverse Adventures:

Embrace the richness of your interests by exploring a spectrum of activities. Whether it's art, nature, or adventure, diversifying your experiences ensures that each date is a new and exciting chapter in your romantic journey.

Surprise Elements:

Infuse an element of surprise into your dates by incorporating small details based on individual preferences. Whether it's a favorite snack, a shared inside joke, or a unique activity, surprises add an extra layer of delight to the experience.

Personalized Touch:

Elevate your date setting by adding small, personal details. Consider creating a playlist of favorite songs, bringing a memento with sentimental value, or incorporating elements that showcase your personality.

Crafting memorable experiences is an art form that goes beyond the ordinary. It's about creating moments that linger in the heart and stand out in the tapestry of your shared history.

Unique Settings:

Venture into unconventional venues that resonate with both of you. Whether it's a rooftop picnic with a breathtaking view, a vintage tram ride through the city, or a lakeside bonfire lounge, unique settings elevate the overall experience.

Shared Adventures:

Engage in activities that foster shared memories, capturing the essence of the moment. From exploring nature trails to attending quirky events, shared adventures create a bond that goes beyond the surface.

Thoughtful Gestures:

Small, thoughtful acts can leave a lasting impact. Consider writing a handwritten note expressing your feelings, planning a surprise related to a shared interest, or incorporating gestures that showcase your thoughtfulness.

Beyond the immediate joy of a personalized date, there's a profound impact on the connection between partners. Let's explore how personalization deepens the emotional bond and contributes to the shared narrative of your relationship.

Emotional Resonance:

Personalized experiences have a unique ability to resonate emotionally. Whether it's revisiting a significant location or recreating a memorable moment, these experiences create a profound connection that lingers.

Understanding and Appreciation:

Tailoring dates showcases a deep understanding and appreciation of each other's preferences. It's a way of saying, "I see you, I understand you, and I value what makes you unique."

Building a Shared Story:

Each personalized date contributes to a shared story, weaving the fabric of your unique connection. These moments become the building blocks of your relationship narrative, creating a bond that stands the test of time.

As you embark on this journey of personalized dating, it's crucial to approach it with intentionality. Tailoring dates is not merely a superficial exercise but a deliberate effort to connect on a deeper level. Let's explore how personalization adds layers of meaning to your dating experiences.

Connection through Intentionality:

Approach personalization with the intention of fostering a deeper connection. Consider the specific preferences, interests, and values that matter to both you and your partner.

Creating Rituals and Traditions:

Personalized dates can evolve into rituals or traditions that strengthen the foundation of your relationship. Whether it's a monthly adventure or an annual celebration, creating consistent experiences builds a sense of continuity.

The Art of Surprise and Delight:

Surprises, when integrated with intentionality, can elevate the overall dating experience. Consider the element of surprise as a tool to express thoughtfulness and keep the relationship dynamic and exciting.

Adapting to Changing Interests:

As individuals grow and evolve, so do their interests. Personalization involves staying attuned to these changes and adapting your dating approach accordingly. Flexibility and openness to new experiences are key.

Now that you understand the significance of personalization, let's delve into practical strategies for success. These tips will guide you in tailoring dates effectively and creating experiences that leave a lasting impression.

Communication is Key:

Open communication is the cornerstone of successful personalization. Discuss interests, preferences, and potential date ideas with your partner. This ensures that your efforts align with their expectations.

Observation and Active Listening:

Pay attention to subtle cues and actively listen to your partner's likes and dislikes. Sometimes, the most personalized ideas stem from everyday conversations and observations.

Balancing Individual and Shared Interests:

While personalization is about celebrating individual interests, finding common ground is equally important. Seek activities that align with both your interests, creating a balanced and inclusive experience.

Surprises Tailored to Personality:

When incorporating surprises, consider your partner's personality. Some may appreciate grand gestures, while others may prefer understated, intimate surprises. Tailor the element of surprise to align with their comfort level.

Personalization emerges as a beacon, guiding you toward a more profound and lasting connection. As you embark on this journey, remember that personalization is not a one-size-fits-all concept. It's about celebrating the uniqueness of your connection and creating experiences that reflect the intricacies of your relationship. May your dates be infused with authenticity, your shared experiences be rich in meaning, and your connection deepen with each personalized adventure. Cheers to the vibrant tapestry of your unique love story!

Navigating Public Spaces

NAVIGATING PUBLIC SPACES bustling with people can be a challenge, especially if you're dealing with anxiety. However, with some strategic tips, you can make these situations more manageable and even enjoyable:

1. **Plan Ahead:**

Knowledge is power. Before heading to a crowded place, familiarize yourself with the layout. Knowing exits, quiet corners, or less crowded areas can provide a sense of control.

1. **Choose Off-Peak Times:**

Timing matters. Opt for times when the place is likely to be less crowded. Early weekdays or late afternoons on weekends are often quieter.

1. **Establish Breaks:**

Plan short breaks during your time in crowded spaces. Having moments to step away, catch your breath, or regroup can prevent overwhelming feelings.

1. **Practice Mindful Breathing:**

Incorporate deep, mindful breathing exercises. Focus on your breath, inhaling and exhaling slowly. This simple technique can help calm nerves in the midst of a crowd.

1. **Communicate with Your Date:**

Openly discuss your feelings with your date. They can offer support, and understanding each other's comfort levels is essential for a successful outing.

Remember, navigating crowded places is about finding a balance that suits you. These tips can empower you to handle anxiety and create an environment where connections can thrive.

Navigating a crowded space can be an exhilarating yet challenging experience, especially when you're trying to maintain a deep connection with your date. In the midst of noise and chaos, strategies for staying focused on each other become invaluable. Here, we break down practical and effective methods to ensure that your connection remains the focal point, making your date memorable and enjoyable.

1. **Non-Verbal Signals:**

Establishing non-verbal signals is like creating your own secret language. A gentle touch on the arm, a shared smile, or a particular gesture can convey volumes without uttering a word. These signals serve as a silent affirmation of your connection, grounding you both in the shared experience.

1. **Active Listening Techniques:**

In the midst of a bustling environment, active listening becomes a superpower. Give your full attention to your date, showing that you are not just hearing but understanding and responding to what they're saying. This not only enhances your connection but also helps you both stay present in the moment.

1. **Shared Experiences:**

Plan activities that facilitate shared experiences. Whether it's sampling street food, exploring an art gallery, or attending a live performance, these joint ventures create lasting memories. Shared experiences strengthen your connection by providing a foundation of shared stories and emotions.

1. **Grounding Techniques:**

Grounding techniques act as an anchor in the storm of distractions. Feel the texture beneath your feet, listen to the ambient sounds, or focus on a specific visual element. Grounding brings you back to the present, helping you stay connected to your date amid the chaos.

1. **Personal Bubble Visualization:**

Imagine a personal bubble enveloping you and your date, creating a mental space that shields you both from the external hustle. This visualization fosters a sense of intimacy while serving as a protective barrier against the surrounding crowd.

1. **Communication Expectations:**

Clear communication about how you both prefer to navigate crowded spaces is crucial. Discuss your communication styles and expectations, ensuring that you're on the same page. This transparency minimizes misunderstandings and maximizes your ability to focus on each other.

In the dance of a crowded space, where distractions abound, employing these strategies can transform your date into a seamlessly connected experience. As you navigate the sea of people, remember that maintaining focus on your connection is not just an art; it's a skill that can turn any crowded outing into a cherished memory.

BALANCING EXPOSURE to social settings is an art, especially when navigating the complexities of dating. The key is to strike a harmonious balance, creating an environment that allows both you and your companion to feel comfortable and engaged. Here are three essential strategies to master this delicate dance:

Choosing the Right Venue:

One of the critical aspects of balancing exposure is selecting the appropriate venue. Consider the size, noise level, and overall atmosphere. Opt for places aligned with your comfort level, such as a cozy café or a quaint bookstore. These environments provide a more intimate setting, allowing for meaningful connection without overwhelming social stimuli.

Establishing Communication Channels:

Effective communication is paramount in navigating social settings. Signal your comfort levels to your date, fostering an open dialogue about each other's preferences. Introduce intentional breaks for moments of quiet and personal reflection. Whether it's stepping outside for fresh air or finding a quiet corner to regroup, these breaks can be invaluable in maintaining a sense of calm and ensuring both parties are at ease.

Adaptability and Socializing Goals:

Understanding the dynamics of socializing requires adaptability. Alternate between intimate, one-on-one venues and slightly more social environments to cater to both introverted and extroverted tendencies. Set realistic expectations for each date, acknowledging that not every outing needs to be a grand social affair. Meaningful connections often blossom in quieter settings, fostering deeper conversations and genuine connections.

Balancing exposure to social settings is a personalized journey, and these strategies aim to provide a roadmap for creating an enjoyable and mutually satisfying dating experience. By implementing these thoughtful approaches, you can navigate social situations with confidence and authenticity.

Congratulations! You've embarked on a journey to transform your dating experiences by delving into the art of selecting comfortable environments. The settings you choose can truly make or break a date, influencing the atmosphere, your mood, and the overall connection with your companion. Let's take a moment to recap the key insights and strategies you've explored in this chapter:

Identifying Ideal Date Locations:

Consider personal comfort preferences when selecting venues. Whether it's a cozy café, a serene park, or an art gallery, choose places that resonate with both you and your date.

Nature as a Calming Element:

Nature has a remarkable ability to soothe the soul. Outdoor date ideas, from sunset blanket lounges to riverside reflections, harness the therapeutic power of nature, creating a relaxed and enjoyable atmosphere.

The Role of Familiarity:

Leveraging familiarity can significantly ease anxiety. Incorporate favorite hangouts into your dates, creating a sense of comfort through shared experiences.

Personalizing the Experience:

Tailoring dates to individual interests and crafting memorable experiences adds a personal touch to your interactions. The impact of this personalization extends beyond the moment, fostering a deeper connection.

Navigating Public Spaces:

Tips for managing anxiety in crowded places, strategies for maintaining focus on the connection, and balancing exposure to social settings provide a toolkit for confidently navigating diverse social landscapes.

As you navigate through this dating adventure, keep in mind that your journey is entirely yours to shape. Embrace the diverse range of experiences, venues, and connections, recognizing that the key lies in discovering what resonates with both you and your date. Confidence in your choices and adaptability to different environments will be your trusted companions.

Your dating experience is a canvas of unique encounters, with each moment contributing to the vibrant palette of meaningful connections. May your future dates be filled with laughter, shared moments, and the joy of genuine connection. Happy dating!

Effective Online Dating Strategies

Chapter 3

"Your passport to a confidence-infused online dating experience is here. Learn the art of crafting an authentic profile, mindful swiping, and mastering the delicate dance from online to offline connections."

Embarking on the online dating journey opens up a world of possibilities, where every swipe could be a step closer to meeting someone special. In this digital realm, crafting a profile that reflects the true you is the first key to success. Picture this: your profile is your digital ambassador, introducing you to potential matches. We'll explore the art of balancing self-expression with authenticity, choosing profile pictures that genuinely reflect your personality, and highlighting your strengths without exaggeration. Remember, honesty is magnetic, and your authenticity will shine through the digital waves.

Swipe right for confidence and let's embark on this adventure together!

Crafting an Authentic Profile

CREATING AN ONLINE dating profile is like crafting your digital identity—a snapshot of who you are and what you're seeking in the vast world of virtual connections. When it comes to Balancing self-expression with authenticity, consider this a delicate dance where you showcase the genuine you without losing sight of your unique personality.

Be Genuine, Be You:

In the realm of online dating, authenticity is magnetic. Begin by presenting a true reflection of yourself. Speak to your passions, interests, and values. Avoid embellishments or projecting an image that doesn't align with who you are. Remember, honesty fosters trust, a fundamental element for meaningful connections.

Showcase Your Personality Through Your Writing Style:

Let your writing style resonate with your personality. If you're witty and light-hearted, infuse your profile with humor. If you're more contemplative, express your thoughts with depth and insight. Use language that feels natural to you; this creates a connection with like-minded individuals who appreciate your unique voice.

Highlight Your Passions with Precision:

When discussing your hobbies or interests, delve into specifics. Instead of merely stating, "I love music," share your favorite genres, artists, or concerts you've attended. Specifics add color to your profile and provide potential matches with meaningful conversation starters.

Choose Words Wisely:

Craft your profile with clarity and brevity. Use succinct language to convey your personality traits and what you're seeking in a partner. Avoid overused clichés and focus on key aspects that set you apart. A clear and concise profile not only captures attention but also makes it easier for others to engage with your narrative.

Strike a Balance Between Humility and Confidence:

While it's essential to highlight your strengths, do so with humility. Avoid coming across as boastful or overly self-assured. Instead of merely listing achievements, share personal anecdotes that illustrate your journey and growth. This humanizes your profile and makes you more relatable.

Invite Conversation:

Conclude your profile with an open invitation for conversation. Encourage potential matches to reach out if they share similar interests or if they appreciate a good discussion. This proactive approach sets the stage for meaningful connections and demonstrates your openness to engaging with others.

In crafting your profile, remember, authenticity is not about perfection; it's about being true to yourself. So, embrace your uniqueness, express it genuinely, and let your profile be the inviting doorway to a world of potential connections.

When it comes to online dating, showcasing your strengths is essential, but it's equally crucial to strike a balance between self-promotion and humility. Highlighting strengths without exaggeration requires finesse and authenticity, ensuring that your profile reflects the best version of yourself without veering into the realm of hyperbole.

Identify Your Unique Strengths:

Begin by identifying your genuine strengths—qualities or skills that define you and contribute positively to your personality. These could be traits like kindness, a sense of humor, creativity, or specific talents. Pinpointing these strengths lays the foundation for an honest portrayal.

Provide Concrete Examples:

Instead of making generic statements about your strengths, support them with concrete examples. If you pride yourself on being a good listener, share a brief story about how you've been there for a friend during a challenging time. Tangible examples offer a more vivid and relatable picture.

Use Thoughtful Language:

The choice of words matters. Craft your profile with thoughtful and descriptive language that communicates your strengths effectively. Instead of simply stating, "I'm adventurous," you might say, "I have a penchant for exploring hidden gems in the city, always up for spontaneous road trips and off-the-beaten-path adventures."

Avoid Superlatives:

While it's natural to want to present your best self, steer clear of using superlatives or absolute statements that may come across as exaggerated. Phrases like "the best" or "always" can undermine the sincerity of your profile. Opt for language that conveys confidence without overstatement.

Share Personal Achievements Modestly:

If you have noteworthy accomplishments, share them modestly. Instead of a boastful list, weave these achievements into your narrative organically. Discuss how these experiences shaped you or contributed to your personal growth. This approach provides context and depth.

Highlight Complementary Strengths:

Consider highlighting strengths that complement the kind of relationship you're seeking. If you value open communication, you might emphasize your ability to express thoughts and feelings. Tailoring your strengths to align with your relationship goals adds relevance to your profile.

Be Open to Growth:

Acknowledge that strengths are not static; they evolve over time. Express openness to personal growth and learning. This humility signals self-awareness and a willingness to adapt, which can be appealing to potential matches.

In crafting a profile that highlights your strengths, remember that authenticity shines brighter than embellishment. By presenting your genuine self with sincerity and thoughtful expression, you create a profile that resonates with those who appreciate you for who you truly are.

SELECTING PROFILE PICTURES for online dating is akin to curating a visual story that conveys your genuine personality. Your photos should go beyond mere aesthetics, offering a glimpse into your life, interests, and, most importantly, your authentic self. Here's a guide on choosing profile pictures that reflect your genuine personality:

1. Showcase Diversity:

- Include a variety of pictures that showcase different facets of your life. Whether it's a candid shot of you immersed in a hobby, a social gathering with friends, or a solo adventure, diversity in photos provides a well-rounded view of your personality.

2. Candid Moments Over Posed Shots:

- While there's a time and place for posed photos, candid shots often capture more authentic moments. Consider including pictures where you're genuinely laughing, engaged in an activity, or lost in thought. These moments offer a more natural and relatable portrayal.

3. Represent Your Interests:

- Incorporate pictures that reflect your hobbies and interests. If you're passionate about hiking, share a photo from a trail. If you love music, include a snapshot from a concert or while playing an instrument. Your profile becomes a visual narrative of what makes you unique.

4. Use Recent Photos:

- Ensure that your profile pictures are recent and accurately represent your current appearance. Authenticity is key, and using outdated photos can create a mismatch between expectations and reality.

5. Capture Genuine Smiles:

- Smiles are universally appealing, and genuine smiles convey warmth and approachability. Opt for pictures where you're authentically smiling, radiating positivity and friendliness.

6. Avoid Overly Edited Images:

- While a touch of editing can enhance a photo, avoid excessive filters or edits that significantly alter your appearance. Transparency is crucial, and potential matches appreciate authenticity over a heavily filtered image.

7. Group Photos with Context:

- If including group photos, provide context or captions to identify who you are in the picture. This helps potential matches understand your social connections and prevents confusion.

8. Pay Attention to Body Language:

- Your body language in photos speaks volumes. Choose pictures where your body language aligns with the message you want to convey. Confidence, approachability, and openness can be communicated through posture and expressions.

9. Balance Solo and Social Photos:

- While solo pictures are essential, including a few social photos can showcase your connections and social life. Strike a balance to avoid an overly solitary or exclusively group-oriented impression.

10. Trust Your Instincts:

- Ultimately, trust your instincts about the vibe each photo conveys. If a picture feels genuine and true to yourself, it's likely to resonate with others. Authenticity fosters a stronger connection with potential matches.

By curating a collection of profile pictures that authentically represent who you are, you set the stage for meaningful connections based on a genuine understanding of your personality and interests.

Mindful Swiping

APPROACHING THE EXPERIENCE with intention is a key factor in creating a positive and meaningful journey. Here's how to navigate the digital realm with purpose:

Setting Clear Intentions

Before delving into the world of online dating, take a moment to reflect on your intentions. Ask yourself what you're looking for in a relationship or connection. Whether it's casual dating, finding a long-term partner, or expanding your social circle, clarifying your goals will guide your actions and decisions.

- **Define Your Relationship Goals:** Clearly articulate what you're seeking, be it companionship, a serious relationship, or simply new friends.

- **Reflect on Personal Readiness**: Ensure that you're emotionally prepared for the potential ups and downs of dating, both online and offline.

Establishing Boundaries for a Positive Experience

Online dating can be overwhelming, and it's essential to set healthy boundaries to safeguard your well-being. Here's how you can establish and maintain boundaries:

- **Define Personal Limits:** Determine the amount of time and energy you're willing to invest in online interactions. This prevents burnout and promotes balance.

- **Be Selective:** Don't feel pressured to respond to every message or match. Prioritize connections that align with your intentions and resonate with you.

- **Communicate Boundaries Clearly:** If there are specific topics or behaviors that make you uncomfortable, communicate these boundaries with potential matches early on.

Recognizing When to Take Breaks

Online dating can become overwhelming at times, and recognizing when to take breaks is crucial for maintaining a positive mindset. It's okay to step back and recharge when needed.

- **Monitor Emotional Well-being:** If you notice signs of stress, fatigue, or frustration, consider taking a break. Your mental and emotional health should always be a priority.

- **Establish Break Triggers:** Identify specific situations or feelings that signal the need for a break. This could include excessive disappointment, fatigue, or a sense of online dating becoming a burden.

- **Engage in Self-Care**: During breaks, focus on self-care activities that rejuvenate you. This might involve pursuing hobbies, spending time with loved ones, or simply enjoying solitude.

Approaching online dating with intention, establishing boundaries, and recognizing the importance of breaks will empower you to navigate the digital dating landscape with confidence and purpose. Remember, the goal is not just to find a connection but to ensure that the journey itself is fulfilling and aligned with your personal growth.

CREATING AND MAINTAINING boundaries is crucial for fostering a positive online dating experience. Here's a detailed exploration of how to set boundaries to ensure your well-being:

1. Time and Energy Boundaries

Why it's important:

Setting limits on the time and energy you invest in online dating prevents burnout and allows you to maintain a healthy balance in your life.

- **Establish Dedicated Time:** Designate specific times for engaging with the app to avoid constant distractions.

- **Set Time Limits:** Limit the duration of each online session to prevent it from consuming your entire day.

- **Prioritize Self-Care:** Ensure that your online dating activities don't compromise your physical and mental well-being.

2. Communication Boundaries

Why it's important:

Clear communication boundaries help manage expectations and create a respectful online environment.

- **Define Response Expectations:** Communicate your preferred response time to manage expectations with matches.

- **Express Comfort Levels:** Clearly convey your comfort levels regarding the pace of communication and the depth of discussions.

- **Be Assertive:** Don't hesitate to assert your boundaries if a conversation becomes uncomfortable or invasive.

3. Personal Information Boundaries

Why it's important:

Protecting your personal information is crucial for your safety and security.

- **Limit Sharing Initially:** Avoid sharing sensitive personal information too soon; let trust develop gradually.

- **Use Caution with Photos:** Be mindful of the images you share and consider privacy settings on the platform.

- **Trust Your Instincts:** If a request for personal information feels uncomfortable, trust your instincts and decline.

4. Emotional Boundaries

Why it's important:

Maintaining emotional boundaries helps protect your emotional well-being and prevents attachment to unrealistic expectations.

- **Be Mindful of Emotional Investment:** Avoid investing too heavily emotionally in the early stages of interaction.

- **Recognize Red Flags:** Pay attention to behaviors or conversations that may indicate emotional manipulation or insincerity.

- **Prioritize Your Needs:** Ensure that your emotional needs are met, both online and offline.

5. Physical Boundaries

Why it's important:

Setting physical boundaries is essential for ensuring your safety and comfort when transitioning from online to offline interactions.

- **Choose Safe Meeting Spaces:** Opt for public places for the first few in-person meetings to ensure safety.

- **Inform Trusted Contacts:** Share your plans with friends or family when meeting someone for the first time.

- **Respect Personal Space:** Clearly communicate and respect personal boundaries when meeting in person.

6. Reassessment and Flexibility

Why it's important:

Being open to reassessing and adjusting boundaries ensures a dynamic and evolving online dating experience.

- Regularly Evaluate Boundaries: Periodically reassess your boundaries based on your experiences and personal growth.

- Be Flexible: Recognize that boundaries may need adjustment as relationships progress or change.

By setting and maintaining these boundaries, you'll create a positive and empowering online dating experience that aligns with your personal well-being and growth. Remember that boundaries are a tool for self-care and a fundamental aspect of building healthy connections.

RECOGNIZING THE NEED for breaks in the realm of online dating is vital for maintaining your mental and emotional well-being. Here's how to identify and honor those moments:

Signs Indicating the Need for a Break

1. Emotional Exhaustion:

- Feeling emotionally drained or overwhelmed by interactions.

- Experiencing heightened anxiety or stress related to online interactions.

2. Decreased Motivation:

- Finding it challenging to engage or losing interest in conversations.
- Not feeling excited or motivated about potential matches or dates.

3. Negative Impact on Mood:

- Noticing a decline in overall mood or experiencing increased negativity.
- Feeling a sense of frustration, disappointment, or pessimism.

4. Loss of Focus on Self-Care:

- Neglecting other aspects of life or feeling a lack of balance.
- Forgetting to engage in activities that usually bring joy or relaxation.

Actions to Take During Breaks

1. Take Time Off:

- Step away from the dating platform for a defined period.
- Engage in activities that recharge and uplift you, focusing on self-care.

2. Reflect and Reassess:

- Reflect on your online dating experiences and assess your emotional state.

- Consider whether adjustments to your approach or boundaries are necessary.

3. Pursue Personal Interests:

- Rediscover hobbies or activities that bring you joy and fulfillment.
- Invest time in nurturing relationships with friends and family.

4. Practice Mindfulness:

- Incorporate mindfulness techniques to alleviate stress and stay present.
- Meditate, practice deep breathing, or indulge in activities that promote mindfulness.

Strategies for Returning Refreshed

1. Set Clear Intentions:

- Establish goals and intentions for re-engaging with online dating.
- Ensure you're mentally prepared and have a positive outlook.

2. Gradual Re-entry:

- Return gradually to the dating platform rather than diving back in fully.
- Ease into interactions and conversations at a comfortable pace.

3. Implement Adjustments:

- Consider implementing changes based on your reflections during the break.

- Adjust boundaries, communication styles, or interaction frequency if needed.

4. Seek Support if Necessary:

- Reach out to friends, a therapist, or a support network if you're feeling overwhelmed.

- Discuss feelings and experiences to gain perspective and support.

Normalizing Breaks as Self-Care

It's essential to recognize that taking breaks is a normal and healthy aspect of online dating. By honoring your emotional state and knowing when to step back, you prioritize your well-being and ensure a more positive and sustainable experience. Remember, breaks aren't a sign of failure but a demonstration of self-awareness and self-care.

Initiating Conversations with Ease

OVERCOMING THE FEAR of the First Message

Initiating the initial message often induces anxiety, but conquering this fear is pivotal for starting conversations with confidence. Acknowledging this nervousness is the first step, normalizing it as a natural part of the process. Embrace imperfection, understanding that genuine connection doesn't hinge on flawless execution but rather on authenticity.

Key Practices:

- **Normalize Nervousness:** Recognize it as common and part of the process.
- **Embrace Imperfection:** Understand that perfection isn't necessary for genuine connection.

Shift your perspective on the first message—view it as an opportunity to share something about yourself or pose an engaging question that sparks conversation. Crafting the message should involve personalization; reference something intriguing from their profile to show sincere interest.

Perspective Shift and Crafting the Message:

- **Focus on Connection, Not Perfection:** Prioritize genuine connection over flawless execution.
- **See It as an Opportunity:** Consider it a chance to share and engage.
- **Personalize the Content:** Reference something specific from their profile.
- **Keep It Simple and Friendly:** Maintain a casual, friendly tone.

To alleviate anxiety, practice drafting multiple versions of the first message. This allows you to choose the one that feels most authentic to your style. Embrace rejection as a part of the process. Reframe rejection as redirection toward someone more aligned with your values.

Anxiety Alleviation Techniques and Handling Rejection:

- **Practice Drafting Messages:** Write several versions and choose the most authentic.
- **Set Realistic Expectations:** Understand not every message leads to a conversation.
- **Reframe Rejection:** View it as redirection to better connections.
- **Learn from Experiences:** Reflect on past interactions for personal growth.

Encourage yourself by celebrating each attempt. Acknowledge the courage it takes to initiate conversations and recognize that it's a continuous learning process.

Encouragement and Self-Compassion:

- **Celebrate Each Attempt:** Acknowledge your bravery in initiating.
- **Practice Self-Compassion:** Be kind to yourself; it's a learning process

.

Overcoming the fear of the first message involves a holistic approach—acknowledging anxiety, shifting perspectives, crafting messages with genuine interest, and embracing the process of connection. The focus is not on perfection but on initiating a dialogue that allows authenticity and connection to unfold naturally.

INITIATING THAT INITIAL contact can be nerve-wracking, but mastering this fear is key to unlocking successful online interactions. Let's break down the process into actionable steps:

Acknowledge the Anxiety:

It's natural to feel jittery about that first message. Acknowledge the anxiety without letting it paralyze you.

Embrace Imperfection:

Perfect is the enemy of good. Understand that your message doesn't need to be flawless. Embrace imperfection as part of the human experience.

Shift Your Perspective:

Instead of viewing it as a daunting task, see the first message as an exciting opportunity to connect with someone new. Focus on the potential for a meaningful conversation.

Personalization is Key:

Tailor your opening line to the individual. Reference something from their profile – a shared interest or a unique detail. Personalization shows genuine interest and effort.

Keep It Simple and Friendly:

A complicated message isn't necessary. Keep your first message simple, friendly, and open-ended. You're not writing a novel; you're starting a conversation.

Practice, Practice, Practice:

Draft several versions of your first message. Practice helps you find your authentic voice and boosts your confidence.

Set Realistic Expectations:

Not every message will result in a lengthy conversation, and that's okay. Set realistic expectations and focus on the act of initiating.

Reframe Rejection:

Instead of viewing a lack of response as rejection, see it as redirection. It's guiding you toward connections more aligned with your interests.

Learn and Grow:

Treat every interaction as a learning experience. Reflect on what works and what doesn't. Use rejection as a stepping stone for personal growth.

Celebrate Your Courage:

Sending that first message takes courage. Celebrate your willingness to step out of your comfort zone and initiate a connection.

Common Mistakes to Avoid When Overcoming the Fear of the First Message

1. Generic Greetings:

- **Mistake:** Starting with a generic "Hey" or "Hi" lacks personalization and often gets lost in a sea of similar messages.

Tailor your greeting to the individual, referencing something specific from their profile to grab their attention.

2. Overthinking and Overcomplicating:

- **Mistake:** Overthinking leads to messages that are too complex or overcomplicated, potentially intimidating the recipient.

Keep it simple. A straightforward and friendly message is more inviting and easier to respond to.

3. Ignoring Personalization:

- Mistake: Sending a message without any reference to the person's profile indicates a lack of effort and genuine interest.

Personalize your message by mentioning shared interests or details from their profile to show you've taken the time to understand them.

4. Being Too Formal:

- **Mistake:** A message that feels overly formal can create a barrier to open communication, making it less inviting.

Maintain a friendly and approachable tone. Remember, it's a conversation, not a business email.

5. Lack of Open-Ended Questions:

- **Mistake:** Closing your message with a statement rather than an open-ended question limits the potential for a flowing conversation.
-

Always end your message with a question that encourages a response and further engagement.

6. Impersonal Compliments:

- **Mistake**: Complimenting physical appearance without any context or personalization may come off as insincere or generic.

Compliment something specific from their profile, such as an achievement or an interest, to make it more genuine.

7. Sending a Novel:

- **Mistake**: Sending a lengthy message in the first interaction can be overwhelming and may discourage the recipient from responding.

Keep your first message concise and engaging. Save in-depth conversations for later.

8. Ignoring Context:

- **Mistake**: Sending a message that doesn't align with the context of their profile or interests may appear disconnected.

Ensure your message reflects an understanding of their profile and aligns with the context of their interests.

9. Overlooking Spelling and Grammar:

- **Mistake**: Messages with frequent spelling or grammatical errors may create a negative impression.

Proofread your message before sending to ensure it's clear, error-free, and easy to understand.

10. Being Too Persistent:

- **Mistake**: Bombarding someone with multiple messages in quick succession after no response can be perceived as pushy.

Allow time for a response before considering a follow-up, and if there's no reply, respect their decision and move on.

Avoiding these common mistakes ensures that your first message is engaging, personalized, and respectful of the recipient's preferences. By steering clear of these pitfalls, you increase the likelihood of initiating a positive and meaningful online interaction.

Personalized Interest:

Example: "Hey [Name], I noticed you're into hiking! I recently conquered [specific trail] and couldn't help but wonder if you have a favorite trail or any hidden gems to recommend?"

Genuine Compliment:

Example: "Hello [Name], I came across your profile and was genuinely impressed by your [specific achievement or hobby]. Your dedication is inspiring! What sparked your interest in [mention the specific interest]?"

Curiosity-Piquing Question:

Example: "Hey [Name], your passion for [specific interest] caught my eye. I'm curious, what's the most memorable experience you've had related to [mention the interest]? I'd love to hear your story!"

Playful Teasing:

Example: "Hi [Name], I stumbled upon your profile and noticed you're a [playful nickname enthusiast]. Do you have a favorite nickname, or should I come up with one for you?"

Remember, the key is to tailor the opening line to the individual's profile and interests for a more personalized and engaging conversation starter.

NAVIGATING THE ONLINE dating landscape isn't just about sending messages—it's about cultivating meaningful connections. Here's your guide to building rapport through genuine interest:

1. **Active Listening in Messages:**

→ Pay close attention to details in their responses.

→ Demonstrates attentiveness and fosters a deeper understanding of their interests.

In the process of building rapport, it's crucial to engage in active listening. Paying close attention to the details in their responses demonstrates your attentiveness, fostering a deeper understanding of their interests. This practice sets the foundation for meaningful connections.

1. **Thoughtful Follow-Up Questions:**

→ Ask follow-up questions based on their previous responses.

→ Shows genuine interest and keeps the conversation flowing.

Thoughtful follow-up questions play a significant role in keeping the conversation dynamic. By asking questions based on their previous responses, you show genuine interest and keep the interaction flowing smoothly. This approach encourages a more in-depth exchange of thoughts and experiences.

1. **Sharing Personal Stories:**

➔ Share anecdotes related to shared interests.

➔ Personal stories create a sense of connection and make conversations more relatable.

Sharing personal stories is a powerful way to create a sense of connection. By relating personal anecdotes to shared interests, you make the conversation more relatable and enjoyable. This openness contributes to a more authentic and engaging dialogue.

1. **Balancing Curiosity Without Prying:**

➔ Ask questions that encourage openness without being intrusive.

➔ Respects boundaries while promoting a deeper understanding of each other.

Balancing curiosity without prying is essential for creating a comfortable atmosphere. Asking questions that encourage openness while respecting boundaries ensures a healthy and respectful exchange. This approach promotes a deeper understanding without making the other person feel uncomfortable.

1. **Expressing Genuine Enthusiasm:**

➔ Express excitement about shared interests or commonalities.

→ Conveys passion and positivity, making the interaction more enjoyable.

Expressing genuine enthusiasm about shared interests is contagious. By conveying your excitement, you contribute to a positive and enjoyable conversation. This shared passion builds a sense of camaraderie and strengthens the connection.

Building rapport through genuine interest involves a mix of active listening, thoughtful questions, and sincere enthusiasm. Combining these practices creates a foundation for more meaningful and authentic relationships, fostering connections that go beyond the surface level.

Moving from Online to Offline

MOVING FROM THE DIGITAL realm to face-to-face interaction is a crucial step in any online connection. Here's your guide on how to discern the opportune moment for this transition:

1. **Establishing a Connection:**

- Building a foundation online involves getting to know each other's interests, values, and communication styles.

- Recognize when you've reached a point where there's a mutual understanding and comfort in your online interactions.

1. **Shared Interests and Values:**

- Look for alignment in your shared interests and values, which can be strong indicators of compatibility.

- When you find common ground and a genuine connection based on these aspects, it might be the right time to consider meeting offline.

1. **Consistent and Engaging Communication:**

- Evaluate the consistency and quality of your online conversations.

- If you find that your communication is both regular and engaging, it's a positive sign that transitioning to in-person dates could be well-received.

1. **Comfort Level:**

- Assess your comfort level with the person through your online interactions.

- When you feel at ease expressing yourself and sharing thoughts, it suggests a strong foundation for taking the connection to the next level.

1. **Expressing Mutual Interest:**

- Pay attention to cues indicating mutual interest in meeting offline.

- If the other person expresses a desire to take the relationship beyond the digital space, it's a clear indication that both parties are open to the idea.

1. **Recognizing Flirtatious or Playful Conversations:**

- Playful banter or flirtatious exchanges can be a sign that there's a dynamic and engaging connection.

- When the conversation naturally takes on a more playful tone, it may be an opportune time to suggest transitioning to in-person dates.

1. **Trust and Transparency:**

- Trust is fundamental in any relationship. Transparency in your online conversations contributes to building trust.

- As trust develops, it becomes easier to broach the subject of meeting face-to-face.

1. **Intuition and Gut Feeling:**

- Trust your intuition. If you feel a positive energy and genuine excitement about the prospect of meeting, it's likely the right time.

- Listen to your gut feeling, as it often provides valuable insights into the timing of transitioning to in-person interactions.

Recognizing the right time to transition to in-person dates involves a combination of building a strong connection, shared interests, consistent communication, and a mutual desire to take the relationship offline. By paying attention to these indicators, you can confidently navigate this transition with a higher likelihood of success.

TAKING THE STEP FROM virtual interactions to a real-life meeting requires thoughtful planning and consideration. Here are strategies to suggest and plan the first date seamlessly:

1. **Be Direct and Confident:**

- **Strategy**: Clearly express your interest in meeting offline.
- **Why**: Directness conveys confidence and sets a positive tone for the suggestion.

Expressing your interest in meeting face-to-face with clarity and confidence is paramount. The strategy of being direct not only eliminates potential misunderstandings but also communicates sincerity and genuine enthusiasm. It sets the stage for a transparent and open interaction, fostering a positive atmosphere as you navigate the transition from virtual to real-life connections.

1. **Propose a Specific Activity:**

- **Strategy**: Suggest a specific activity or venue for the first date.
- **Why**: Having a concrete plan demonstrates intentionality and makes the proposition more appealing.

When suggesting the first date, proposing a specific activity or venue goes beyond a generic invitation. It showcases thoughtfulness and intentionality, giving the other person a clear idea of what to expect. This strategy not only adds a layer of excitement but also makes the proposition more attractive, as it shows you've put thought into creating an enjoyable and memorable experience.

1. **Consider Shared Interests:**

- **Strategy**: Plan an activity aligned with shared interests.

- **Why**: A date centered around common hobbies ensures a more enjoyable and engaging experience.

Aligning the first date with shared interests is a powerful strategy for creating a connection from the outset. By incorporating activities both individuals enjoy, the date becomes more than just a meeting—it becomes an opportunity to bond over mutual passions. This approach ensures a more engaging and enjoyable experience, setting the foundation for a potential deeper connection.

1. **Choose a Comfortable Venue:**

- **Strategy:** Select a venue that is comfortable and conducive to conversation.

- **Why:** Comfort is essential for creating a relaxed atmosphere during the first meeting.

The choice of venue plays a pivotal role in the success of a first date. Opting for a comfortable and conversation-friendly setting creates an atmosphere that encourages open communication. This strategy prioritizes the ease and comfort of both individuals, setting the stage for a relaxed and enjoyable initial encounter.

1. **Consider Daytime Options:**

- **Strategy**: Opt for daytime activities for a casual and less pressured environment.

- **Why**: Daytime dates can feel more relaxed and offer flexibility in terms of scheduling.

Choosing daytime activities as a strategy for the first date introduces a more laid-back and casual vibe. Daytime settings tend to be less pressured, allowing both individuals to feel more at ease. This approach not only provides flexibility in scheduling but also contributes to a comfortable and enjoyable atmosphere, fostering a positive initial meeting.

NAVIGATING THE REALM of first dates requires a delicate balance of excitement and grounded expectations. Rather than scripting the perfect encounter, embracing the unpredictability of the moment sets the stage for genuine connection. Expect imperfections, prioritize authenticity, and shift the focus from an idealized outcome to the joy of building a meaningful connection.

Tips for Managing Expectations:

1. **Embrace Uncertainty Mindfully:**

- Ground yourself in the present, appreciating each moment without overanalyzing or projecting too far into the future. Mindful acceptance of uncertainty fosters a positive mindset.

1. **Cultivate Authenticity Over Perfection:**

- Understand that authenticity resonates more than perfection. Embracing imperfections in yourself and your date creates an environment conducive to genuine connection.

1. **Communicate Openly and Honestly:**

- Foster transparent communication about expectations. Share your thoughts and encourage your date to do the same, creating a shared understanding of what each person hopes to gain from the experience.

Tips for Managing Nervousness:

Navigating nervousness is an intrinsic part of first dates, but employing practical strategies can ease the tension and contribute to a more enjoyable experience.

1. **Practice Deep Breathing Techniques:**

- Incorporate deep breathing exercises to calm nerves. Inhale slowly, hold, and exhale to regulate anxiety and promote a sense of calm.

1. **Visualize a Positive Outcome:**

- Picture a positive and enjoyable outcome before the date. Visualization helps shift your mindset, alleviating nervousness and fostering optimism.

1. **Arrive Early and Familiarize Yourself:**

- Arrive a bit early to familiarize yourself with the surroundings. This not only eases initial nervousness but also allows you to settle into the environment before your date arrives.

Navigating the intricacies of first dates involves maintaining a healthy perspective on expectations while employing practical tips to manage nervousness. Embrace the spontaneity of the experience, cultivate authenticity, and approach the date with an open mind, understanding that connections often flourish in the midst of unpredictability.

Dealing with Online Rejection

IN THE DIGITAL DATING landscape, mastering the art of resilience amid online rejection is crucial. Uncover coping mechanisms, reframe setbacks as redirection, and harness rejection for personal growth in this insightful guide, navigating the intricacies of virtual connections with grace and empowerment.

Coping Mechanisms for Handling Rejection:

Navigating rejection in the realm of online dating demands resilience and emotional fortitude. Here are pivotal coping mechanisms to gracefully navigate these challenging moments:

1. **Cultivate Emotional Awareness:**

- Acknowledge and process emotions without judgment.
- Reflect on feelings to foster emotional intelligence.

Acknowledging and understanding your emotional responses to rejection forms the cornerstone of resilience. Embracing emotions without judgment allows for a deeper understanding of yourself, fostering emotional growth.

1. **Foster Supportive Connections:**

- Seek solace in a supportive network of friends or community.
- Share experiences and gain varied perspectives for comfort and solidarity.

Surrounding yourself with supportive individuals offers comfort during moments of rejection. Sharing experiences and perspectives fosters a sense of camaraderie and solidarity, alleviating the burden of rejection.

1. **Practice Self-Compassion:**

- Extend kindness and understanding toward yourself.
- Treat personal struggles with the same empathy as you would a friend's.

Embracing self-compassion is pivotal in handling rejection. Being kind and understanding to yourself softens the emotional impact, enabling a more resilient response to setbacks.

NAVIGATING REJECTION in the realm of online dating demands a profound shift in perspective—a transformation where setbacks are not seen as roadblocks but rather as guiding lights toward a more aligned path. Reframing rejection as redirection is a mindset that transcends disappointment, offering a profound opportunity for personal growth and self-discovery.

Embracing the Path of Self-Discovery:

Rejection often feels like a dead end, a closure to a potential connection. However, this mindset perceives rejection as a detour—one that diverts you towards a path of self-discovery and growth. It's an acknowledgment that not every connection is meant to flourish but that each encounter holds invaluable lessons. By embracing rejection as redirection, you open yourself to the possibility of uncovering deeper insights about yourself and what truly resonates with your aspirations and values.

Identifying Lessons and Opportunities:

Redirection through rejection is not a termination but a pivot towards opportunities. It's about recognizing the lessons embedded within the disappointment. Each rejection holds insights into compatibility, communication, and personal preferences. By deciphering these lessons, rejection transforms into a guiding force—a compass pointing towards connections that resonate more authentically with your journey. It's an opportunity to align more closely with what truly matters to you.

Fostering a Growth Mindset:

The crux of reframing rejection as redirection lies in fostering a growth mindset. It's about viewing challenges not as setbacks but as catalysts for learning and adaptation. Each rejection becomes a classroom—a place to nurture resilience and evolve. Embracing rejection with a growth mindset cultivates adaptability, allowing you to approach future connections with renewed understanding and wisdom garnered from past experiences.

This transformation in perception not only alters the way rejection is perceived but also redefines the narrative surrounding it. It's about shifting the focus from what's lost to what's gained. Rejection no longer signifies failure but becomes a stepping stone toward self-improvement and a more aligned future.

By reframing rejection as redirection, individuals embarking on the online dating journey can harness the power of disappointment. It becomes less about the end of a connection and more about the redirection towards better-suited opportunities. This shift empowers individuals to navigate rejection with grace, resilience, and a heightened sense of self-awareness.

In this journey of transformation, it's crucial to internalize these principles as a continuous process. Rejection becomes not a roadblock but a pivotal part of a greater narrative—a narrative of growth, self-discovery, and ultimately, the discovery of connections that resonate more authentically with who you are and who you aspire to be.

REJECTION IS NOT AN endpoint but a classroom for personal growth. Here's how to leverage rejection as a powerful tool for self-improvement:

1. **Embrace the Feedback Loop:**

- See rejection as feedback rather than failure.
- Extract constructive insights from the reasons communicated or implied.

Rejection becomes a feedback loop—an opportunity to refine your approach. By shifting the focus from failure to feedback, you transform rejection into a valuable source of insights, helping you understand what aspects may need adjustment.

1. **Reflect on Personal Values:**

- Assess whether rejection aligns with your values.
- Use rejection as a catalyst for refining and reaffirming your core values.

Rejection provides a moment to reflect on compatibility with your values. Use this as an opportunity to reassess and refine your core values, ensuring future connections align more authentically with your aspirations.

1. **Identify Areas for Personal Development:**

- Recognize patterns or recurring themes in rejections.

- View these patterns as indicators of potential areas for personal development.

Repeated rejections may point to specific patterns. Use these patterns as signposts for personal development, fostering a proactive approach toward refining aspects of yourself that could contribute to more positive connections.

1. **Strengthen Emotional Resilience:**

- Develop resilience by facing rejection with a growth mindset.

- Cultivate an understanding that rejection does not diminish your worth.

Building emotional resilience is key to transforming rejection into a catalyst for growth. Adopting a growth mindset allows you to see rejection as a temporary setback, acknowledging that it does not diminish your inherent value.

1. **Channel Rejection into Motivation:**

- Use rejection as fuel for personal motivation.

- Set realistic goals for self-improvement based on rejection insights.

Rather than letting rejection deter you, channel it into motivation for self-improvement. Set achievable goals based on insights gained from rejections, fostering a proactive approach toward personal growth.

Leveraging rejection for personal growth is about turning setbacks into stepping stones. It's an intentional process that transforms the sting of rejection into an opportunity for self-reflection and improvement. By approaching rejection with a growth-oriented mindset, each experience becomes a valuable chapter in the narrative of your personal development—a journey that ultimately leads to more meaningful connections and a heightened sense of self.

IN THE QUEST FOR CONFIDENT and authentic online connections, this chapter provided a roadmap. From crafting genuine profiles to navigating the transition from pixels to reality, these strategies aim to elevate your digital dating experience. As we conclude, you're equipped to turn every click into a meaningful connection. Ready for the next chapter in your dating adventure? Let's dive in.

1. **Crafting an Authentic Profile:**

- Balance self-expression with authenticity.
- Highlight strengths genuinely, avoiding exaggeration.
- Choose profile pictures that authentically reflect your personality.

1. **Mindful Swiping:**

- Approach online dating with intention.
- Set boundaries for a positive and enriching experience.
- Recognize when it's time to take breaks for your well-being.

1. **Initiating Conversations with Ease:**

• Overcome the fear of the first message with confidence.

• Tailor opening lines to resonate with the individual.

• Build rapport through genuine interest and meaningful conversation.

1. **Moving from Online to Offline:**

• Recognize the opportune time to transition to in-person dates.

• Employ effective strategies for suggesting and planning the first date.

• Manage expectations and nervousness, ensuring a smooth transition.

1. **Dealing with Online Rejection:**

• Employ coping mechanisms to handle rejection gracefully.

• Reframe rejection as redirection, embracing it as a guide toward personal growth.

• Extract valuable lessons from rejection experiences for continuous self-improvement.

This chapter equips you with the tools and insights needed to navigate the complexities of online dating. From crafting an authentic profile that genuinely represents you to seamlessly transitioning from pixels to real-life connections, these strategies aim to enhance your confidence and make your online dating experience both enjoyable and growth-oriented. Whether you're a novice or a seasoned dater, these takeaways provide a roadmap for building meaningful connections in the digital age.

Mastering Conversation Skills

Chapter 4

"Ready to turn ordinary conversations into extraordinary connections? Explore the art of dialogue with us and learn how to navigate silences, making each moment count."

Embark on a journey where conversations transcend the ordinary and become extraordinary connections. In this exploration, we delve into the intricate art of dialogue, uncovering the secrets that transform mere words into bridges of understanding. Navigating the pauses and silences becomes an art form, where each moment carries significance. Join us in mastering the skill of engaging conversation, where every exchange is an opportunity to deepen connections and create moments that resonate long after the words have been spoken.

The Art of Active Listening

BEING FULLY PRESENT in conversations is a skill that transforms dialogue into a meaningful exchange. Here are techniques to help you immerse yourself in the moment:

1. **Mindful Focus:** Direct your attention to the speaker, blocking out distractions. Maintain eye contact to signal your engagement.

1. **Silencing the Inner Commentary:** Quiet the internal chatter. Avoid formulating responses while the speaker is talking, allowing yourself to absorb their words without interruption.

1. **Non-Verbal Cues:** Utilize body language to convey attentiveness. Nodding, leaning slightly forward, and mirroring expressions signal your involvement in the conversation.

1. **Active Participation:** Engage by responding appropriately. Share affirmations, ask questions, and provide feedback to show you are actively processing the information.

1. **Limiting Multitasking:** Minimize distractions by focusing solely on the conversation. Put away devices and avoid multitasking, ensuring your attention is dedicated to the speaker.

Being fully present lays the foundation for genuine connections, fostering an environment where conversations are not just heard but truly felt.

1. **Mindful Focus:**

In the realm of active listening, your compass is mindful focus. It's not merely about hearing words; it's about immersing yourself in the present moment and fully understanding the speaker's perspective.

a. **Direct Your Attention:** Focus your gaze on the speaker, blocking out potential distractions.
b. **Silence the Inner Commentary:** Resist the urge to formulate responses while the speaker is talking. Allow their words to unfold without interruption.

1. **Non-Verbal Cues:**

Your body language becomes the unspoken language of connection. Employing non-verbal cues not only enhances the conversation but also fosters a deeper understanding between you and the speaker.

a. **Maintain Eye Contact:** Establish a connection by looking directly at the speaker, showing your undivided attention.
b. **Nodding:** A subtle nod can affirm that you are actively processing the information and encourage the speaker to continue.

a. **Mirroring Expressions:** Reflect the speaker's emotions through subtle mirroring, creating a sense of shared understanding.

1. **Active Participation:**

Actively participating in a conversation goes beyond being a passive listener. It involves responding in a way that contributes to the dynamic exchange of ideas, ensuring a more engaging and meaningful interaction.

a. **Respond Appropriately:** Provide affirmations, ask questions, and offer thoughtful feedback to convey your understanding and engagement.
b. **Thoughtful Questions:** Pose questions that encourage depth and openness, demonstrating a genuine interest in the speaker's perspective.
c. **Feedback:** Offer constructive feedback to show that you are not only hearing but also actively processing and responding to the speaker's words.

1. **Empathy in Action:**

Empathy transforms active listening from a skill into a powerful tool for connection. It involves stepping into the speaker's shoes, understanding not only their words but also their emotions and experiences.

a. **Feel Their Emotions:** Try to genuinely feel and understand the emotions conveyed by the speaker.
b. **Express Understanding:** Use verbal and non-verbal cues to express your understanding of the speaker's emotional state.
c. **Validate Emotions:** Acknowledge the legitimacy of the

speaker's emotions, fostering a deeper emotional connection.

1. **Connecting Through Validation:**

Validation is a cornerstone of active listening. It goes beyond merely hearing; it involves confirming the speaker's thoughts and feelings, creating a space where they feel truly understood.

a. **Verbal Acknowledgment:** Use affirming statements to validate the speaker's perspective.
b. **Reflective Responses:** Mirror the speaker's words to confirm your understanding of their viewpoint.
c. **Avoid Judgments:** Refrain from passing judgments, ensuring the speaker feels accepted and valued.

By integrating these techniques into your active listening repertoire, you create a foundation for more profound and meaningful connections in your interactions.

ACTIVE LISTENING, A cornerstone of effective communication, demands a nuanced approach to overcome common pitfalls that can impede meaningful engagement. One crucial pitfall to sidestep is the inclination to interrupt. Patience becomes a virtuous ally, allowing the speaker the necessary space to articulate their thoughts without disruption. Additionally, resisting the temptation to formulate responses prematurely is paramount. By embracing the silence between words, you create room for genuine understanding to flourish. Another pitfall to navigate is avoiding confirmation bias. Recognizing and challenging your pre-existing beliefs opens the door to a more open and unbiased exchange, enriching conversations with diverse perspectives.

Key Strategies:

1. **Resist Interrupting:**

- **Practice Patience:** Cultivate the habit of patiently allowing the speaker to express themselves fully before responding.

- **Embrace Silence:** Recognize the power of silence as a tool for fostering deeper understanding and connection.

- **Value the Speaker's Voice:** Acknowledge the importance of every word uttered by the speaker, demonstrating respect for their perspective.

1. **Avoid Premature Responses:**

- **Listen Actively:** Focus on actively listening to the speaker rather than formulating responses while they speak.

- **Promote Understanding:** Prioritize understanding over the need to offer immediate replies, fostering a deeper connection.

- **Create Mental Space:** Clear mental space for the speaker's words to resonate, ensuring a more thoughtful response.

1. **Challenge Confirmation Bias:**

- **Recognize Biases:** Acknowledge and identify personal biases that may influence your interpretation of the speaker's message.

- **Seek Diverse Perspectives:** Actively seek out diverse perspectives to counteract confirmation bias and promote inclusive dialogue.

- **Encourage Openness:** Foster an environment where differing opinions are welcomed, allowing for a more comprehensive exchange of ideas.

By navigating these pitfalls with intentionality, you pave the way for enhanced connections through active presence, transforming each conversation into a collaborative and enriching experience.

Asking Thoughtful Questions

MEANINGFUL CONVERSATIONS require the skill of asking questions that transcend the superficial. Crafting queries that encourage depth and openness is akin to unlocking a door to richer, more authentic exchanges. It involves the art of inquiry that goes beyond the mundane, inviting individuals to share the intricacies of their thoughts and experiences.

Strategies for Crafting Questions:

1. **Probe Emotions:**

- **Explore Feelings:** Pose questions that delve into the emotional landscape, encouraging the speaker to express nuanced sentiments.

- **Facilitate Self-Reflection:** Ask about personal experiences that prompt individuals to reflect on their emotional responses.

Instead of asking, "What did you do this weekend?" inquire, "Can you share a moment that brought you joy or challenged you emotionally?"

1. **Encourage Storytelling:**

- **Narrative-Centric Questions:** Craft inquiries that prompt storytelling, inviting individuals to share their experiences in narrative form.

- **Highlight Significant Moments:** Ask about pivotal moments in their lives, allowing for a deeper understanding of personal narratives.

Instead of a standard, "How was your day?" inquire, "Can you recount a specific moment from today that left a lasting impression?"

1. **Explore Values and Beliefs:**

- **Delve into Personal Values:** Pose questions that encourage individuals to discuss their core values and belief systems.

- **Connect Values to Experiences:** Explore how their values align with past experiences, fostering a deeper understanding of their perspectives.

Rather than a generic, "What do you do?" inquire, "How does your profession align with your personal values?"

1. **Temporal Reflection:**

- **Past, Present, Future:** Structure questions that prompt individuals to reflect on their past, engage with the present, or envision the future.

- **Extract Learnings:** Encourage discussions on how past experiences have shaped their present mindset or influenced future aspirations.

Instead of a standard, "What are your hobbies?" inquire, "How have your past interests contributed to who you are today, and what do you envision for your future passions?"

1. **Aspirations and Dreams:**

- **Futuristic Inquiry:** Pose questions that invite individuals to share their aspirations, dreams, and long-term goals.

- **Encourage Visionary Thinking:** Explore how their dreams contribute to their sense of purpose and influence their life journey.

Rather than a casual, "Where do you see yourself in five years?" inquire, "Can you describe a dream or aspiration that profoundly influences your life choices?"

1. **Reflective Challenges:**

- **Navigate Challenges:** Craft questions that prompt individuals to reflect on challenges they've faced and the lessons learned.

- **Encourage Growth Narratives:** Explore how overcoming challenges has contributed to personal growth and resilience.

Instead of asking, "How do you handle stress?" inquire, "Can you share a specific challenge you've faced and the ways it has shaped your resilience and personal development?"

Crafting questions that encourage depth and openness is an art form that transforms ordinary conversations into meaningful dialogues. By adopting these strategies, you empower yourself to navigate the profound layers of human connection through intentional and thought-provoking inquiry.

CURIOSITY, AKIN TO a gentle breeze that stirs the waters of conversation, plays a pivotal role in fostering deep and meaningful connections. It is the magnetic force that draws individuals into the depths of understanding, unraveling layers of thoughts, experiences, and emotions. In exploring "The role of curiosity in fostering connection," we uncover the transformative power of genuine inquisitiveness in building authentic relationships.

Curiosity serves as the catalyst for meaningful connections, propelling conversations beyond the surface. It sparks a genuine interest in understanding the intricacies of another person's perspective, creating a foundation for profound dialogue. This innate human quality cultivates an environment where individuals feel seen, heard, and valued.

Active Engagement:

- **Probing Interest:** Genuine curiosity manifests through intentional questions that delve into the nuances of another person's experiences and viewpoints.

- **Demonstrating Presence:** Curiosity requires active engagement, necessitating attentive listening and a genuine desire to comprehend the unique narrative of the other.

Curiosity forms a bridge to empathy, allowing individuals to step into the shoes of others and comprehend their emotions. It challenges assumptions, fostering a culture where preconceived notions give way to a more nuanced understanding of individual stories.

Bridge to Empathy:

- **Empathetic Understanding:** Curiosity forms a bridge to empathy, allowing individuals to step into the shoes of others and comprehend their emotions.

- **Breaking Assumptions:** It challenges assumptions, fostering a culture where preconceived notions give way to a more nuanced understanding of individual stories.

Curiosity finds its expression through thoughtful questioning, steering conversations toward meaningful and transformative terrain. It invites individuals to explore not only the external facets of their lives but also the internal landscapes of thoughts, feelings, and aspirations.

Open-Ended Inquiry:

- **Encouraging Exploration:** Curiosity thrives on open-ended questions that invite expansive answers, allowing individuals to explore and share their thoughts freely.

- **Example:** Instead of a closed question like, "Did you enjoy your vacation?" a curious inquiry might be, "What aspects of your recent vacation brought you the most joy, and why?"

Embracing the Unknown:

- **Welcoming Novelty:** Curiosity embraces the unknown, encouraging individuals to discuss topics beyond the familiar and venture into unexplored territories.

- **Example:** Instead of sticking to routine queries, a curious approach might involve asking, "Is there a topic or hobby you've always wanted to explore but haven't had the chance to? What draws you to it?"

In essence, the role of curiosity in fostering connection lies in its ability to transform conversations into shared explorations. By embracing the unknown, actively engaging with others, and using open-ended questions, curiosity becomes the cornerstone of authentic relationships, creating a tapestry woven with the threads of genuine understanding and connection.

STRIKING A DELICATE balance between curiosity and respect is paramount. "Balancing curiosity without prying" is an art that requires finesse, understanding, and a genuine regard for the boundaries of others. As we explore this delicate equilibrium, we unveil the essence of respectful curiosity and its role in nurturing relationships.

Curiosity, when wielded with finesse, becomes a tool for building bridges rather than dismantling walls. It involves navigating the labyrinth of inquiry with an acute awareness of the comfort zones and personal boundaries of those we engage with.

Respecting Boundaries:

- **Mindful Inquiry:** Balancing curiosity involves asking questions with mindfulness, considering the potential impact on the other person's comfort and privacy.

- **Example:** Instead of prying into personal matters, a respectful inquiry might be, "If you're comfortable sharing, what led you to choose your career path?"

Curiosity, when infused with sensitivity, respects the autonomy of others. It refrains from digging too deep into private matters and acknowledges that certain topics may be off-limits or require a more gradual approach.

Sensitive Pacing:

- **Gradual Exploration:** Balancing curiosity involves pacing the exploration of topics in a way that aligns with the other person's comfort level.

- **Example:** Instead of delving into sensitive personal experiences immediately, a balanced approach might be, "I'm genuinely interested in learning more about your journey. If and when you feel comfortable, I'd love to hear more about your experiences."

In the realm of respectful curiosity, active listening becomes a guiding light. It involves tuning into verbal and non-verbal cues, allowing the other person's comfort or discomfort to shape the trajectory of the conversation.

Active Listening:

- **Reading Cues:** Balancing curiosity requires attentiveness to the cues provided by the other person, allowing their responses to guide the direction of the conversation.

- **Example:** If someone expresses hesitation or discomfort, a respectful response might be, "I appreciate your honesty. We can shift the conversation to a different topic that feels more comfortable for you."

Curiosity, when balanced with sensitivity, becomes a bridge that connects rather than a force that intrudes. It reflects an understanding that genuine connection flourishes in an environment of mutual respect, where each individual feels seen, heard, and valued.

The art of "Balancing curiosity without prying" lies in navigating the landscape of inquiry with a compass of sensitivity and respect.

Sharing Personal Stories

IN THE TAPESTRY OF meaningful connections, the art of opening up during conversations is akin to weaving threads of vulnerability and authenticity. This section explores strategies that pave the way for genuine self-expression, fostering an environment where individuals feel comfortable sharing their thoughts, feelings, and experiences.

1. **Gradual Self-Disclosure:**

• **Start Small:** Opening up doesn't require divulging the most intimate details immediately. Begin with sharing small anecdotes or personal preferences to create a sense of comfort.

• **Example:** Instead of revealing a deep personal story, start by sharing a favorite hobby or a memorable experience from your day.

Gradual self-disclosure involves a phased approach, allowing individuals to reveal more about themselves as trust and rapport develop within the conversation.

1. **Reflective Listening:**

- **Empathetic Engagement:** Encourage openness by actively listening to the other person's thoughts and responding with empathy. Reflecting on what they share fosters an environment of reciprocal sharing.

- **Example:** After someone shares a challenging experience, respond with empathy by saying, "I appreciate you sharing that with me. It sounds like it was a significant moment for you."

Reflective listening creates a space for individuals to feel heard and understood, laying the foundation for mutual openness.

1. **Share Personal Insights:**

- **Lead by Example:** Demonstrate openness by sharing personal insights and reflections. This vulnerability invites reciprocity and encourages others to express themselves more freely.

- **Example**: Before asking a personal question, share a relevant personal experience, creating an atmosphere of shared vulnerability.

Leading by example breaks down barriers and sets the tone for an open and honest exchange of thoughts and feelings.

1. **Create a Judgment-Free Zone:**

- **Embrace Acceptance:** Communicate a non-judgmental stance, assuring individuals that their thoughts and feelings are valued without fear of criticism.

- **Example**: Affirming statements like, "I appreciate your honesty, and there's no judgment here," create a safe space for open dialogue.

Fostering a judgment-free zone dismantles inhibitions, making it more comfortable for individuals to express themselves authentically.

1. **Ask Open-Ended Questions:**

- **Encourage Thoughtfulness:** Frame questions in a way that invites detailed responses, steering away from yes or no answers. This encourages individuals to delve deeper into their thoughts and experiences.

- **Example:** Instead of asking, "Did you enjoy your weekend?" pose a more open-ended question like, "What highlights from your weekend brought you joy?"

Asking open-ended questions stimulates thoughtful responses, fostering a conversational environment where depth and authenticity flourish.

Discovering Common Interests

Ellie: Hi, River! Nice to finally meet you. How's your day been?

River: Hey, Ellie! It's good, thanks. A bit nervous about this whole setup, though.

Ellie: Oh, trust me, I totally get the nerves. But hey, your profile mentioned you're into music. What do you play?

River: I'm all about the guitar. Big fan of Megadeth. Work at an office job, but music's my real passion.

Ellie: That's pretty cool! I've always admired guitarists; it's such a versatile instrument. What do you love about playing?

River: Well, there's this freedom in strumming those strings. Makes the office hours seem a bit less mundane, you know?

Ellie: Absolutely! There's something magical about music. I've been learning a bit about different instruments. What's your favorite Megadeth song to play?

River: "Symphony of Destruction" usually gets the fingers moving. How about you? Any musical interests?

Ellie: Not exactly, but I'm curious. I've been reading up on how music influences people's moods. Any song recommendations?

River: Well, Megadeth's got some intense tracks, but they're not for everyone. Maybe start with "A Tout le Monde" for something mellower?

Ellie: That sounds intriguing, I'll give it a listen. By the way, working in an office, do you find time for music?

River: It's tricky, but I squeeze in practice whenever I can. It's like my own little therapy session after work.

Ellie: I can imagine! Music has a way of unwinding the day's stress. Speaking of which, have you been to any live gigs lately?

River: Not recently, but I'm always on the lookout. The energy at live shows is something else.

Ellie: Absolutely! Well, you'll have to let me know when you catch your next gig. I'd love to hear about it.

OPENING UP IN A CONVERSATION involves a delicate dance between sharing personal stories and respecting individual comfort levels. It's crucial to approach vulnerability with authenticity, allowing the conversation to unfold naturally.

Respecting comfort zones is key. Pay attention to verbal and non-verbal cues, ensuring that both parties feel at ease. This creates a conducive environment for openness without imposing pressure.

Incremental trust-building is a gradual process. Share personal experiences at a pace that feels comfortable, fostering a safe space for mutual vulnerability. This approach ensures a secure and evolving connection over time.

Establishing clear boundaries is essential. Communicate openly about off-limit topics and areas that require more time before delving into. This promotes mutual understanding and control over the depth of disclosure.

Reciprocal sharing enhances connection. Encourage the other person to share in return, creating a balanced exchange. This mutual contribution deepens connections, establishing a foundation for trust and authenticity.

In summary, navigating vulnerability and privacy requires intentional and respectful sharing. Cultivate an environment that promotes comfortable self-expression, allowing connections to flourish with depth and authenticity.

Connection is the heartbeat of any relationship, and shared experiences serve as the glue that binds individuals together. The journey of building a strong connection involves creating and cherishing moments that resonate with both parties.

Creating Meaningful Memories:

Shared experiences become the building blocks of lasting memories. Engaging in activities together, whether big or small, forges a connection based on shared joy, laughter, and discovery. These shared moments create a reservoir of positive memories that deepen the bond over time.

Authenticity in Shared Experiences:

The authenticity of shared experiences adds richness to relationships. When individuals are true to themselves in the shared moments, it fosters a genuine connection. This authenticity creates a sense of safety and acceptance, allowing both parties to be vulnerable and truly seen.

Navigating Challenges Together:

Facing challenges as a team strengthens the connection. Whether it's overcoming obstacles during an adventure or navigating life's twists and turns, shared experiences build resilience. The mutual support and understanding developed through these challenges fortify the foundation of a strong connection.

Celebrating Milestones:

Shared experiences mark significant milestones in a relationship. Celebrating achievements, no matter how small, enhances the connection by acknowledging each other's growth and successes. These celebratory moments contribute to a positive and affirming relationship dynamic.

Building Traditions and Rituals:

Creating shared traditions and rituals establishes a sense of continuity and predictability. Whether it's a weekly movie night, an annual getaway, or a special anniversary celebration, these rituals provide a comforting rhythm to the relationship, fostering a sense of belonging and shared history.

Building a connection through shared experiences involves actively participating in each other's lives, embracing authenticity, navigating challenges together, celebrating milestones, and establishing meaningful traditions. These shared moments not only create a strong connection today but also contribute to the foundation of a lasting and fulfilling relationship.

Navigating Awkward Silences

IN THE SYMPHONY OF conversation, silence is the pause that adds depth and nuance to the melody. Contrary to popular belief, silence is not an awkward void but a natural and integral part of meaningful communication. Embracing these pauses can transform the dynamics of a conversation, allowing for a deeper understanding and connection between individuals.

Understanding the Power of Silence:

Silence is a potent communicative tool that allows for reflection and introspection. Rather than viewing it as an uncomfortable void, consider it a moment to absorb, process, and respond thoughtfully. Embracing silence fosters a more profound connection by giving each person the mental space to express themselves genuinely.

Creating Space for Reflection:

Silence provides a canvas for reflection, allowing individuals to ponder and articulate their thoughts more clearly. By embracing these pauses, you create an environment where both parties feel comfortable expressing themselves without the pressure of immediate responses. This reflective space enhances the quality of the exchange.

Non-Verbal Communication:

Silence speaks volumes through non-verbal cues. Facial expressions, body language, and subtle gestures convey emotions and sentiments that words may not capture. Embracing silence encourages individuals to be attuned to these non-verbal cues, fostering a deeper understanding of each other's emotions and perspectives.

Cultivating Comfort in Silence:

Anxiety around silence often stems from societal expectations of continuous chatter. By embracing silence as a natural and positive aspect of conversation, individuals can cultivate comfort in being present with each other without the need for constant verbal interaction. This comfort contributes to a more authentic and relaxed connection.

Mindful Listening in Silence:

Silent moments invite mindful listening. Rather than focusing on formulating responses, individuals can attentively listen to the nuances within the silence. This mindful listening enhances comprehension, allowing for a more empathetic and considerate exchange of ideas.

Embracing silence as a natural part of conversation transforms it from an uncomfortable void into a powerful tool for reflection, non-verbal communication, and mindful listening. By fostering an environment where silence is welcomed, individuals can deepen their connection and enrich the quality of their interactions.

Let's explore effective techniques for gracefully handling those inevitable awkward pauses in conversations. Here are strategies to help you navigate these moments seamlessly:

1. **Mindful Breathing:**

- Take a deep breath during a pause.
- Use this moment to center yourself and maintain composure.

1. **Maintain Positive Body Language:**

- Smile gently to convey warmth.
- Avoid appearing tense; relax your shoulders and maintain eye contact.

1. **Use Humor:**

- Lightly inject humor into the situation.
- A well-timed, light-hearted comment can diffuse tension.

1. **Redirect the Conversation:**

- Seamlessly transition to a related or new topic.
- Guide the conversation toward shared interests or experiences.

1. **Validate the Silence:**

- Acknowledge the pause without discomfort.
- A simple "Let's take a moment to think about that" can create a natural break.

1. **Ask Open-Ended Questions:**

- Encourage the other person to share more.

- Open-ended questions invite depth and keep the conversation flowing.

1. **Share a Personal Anecdote:**

- Relate an anecdote or story relevant to the discussion.
- Personal stories add a layer of authenticity to the interaction.

1. **Express Understanding:**

- If the pause follows a statement, show empathy.
- Express understanding with a nod or a thoughtful response.

Remember, awkward silences are a natural part of any conversation. Embracing these moments with grace and employing these techniques will not only make you more comfortable but also create an atmosphere where genuine connections can thrive.

Setting: A Cozy Café

John and Emma, both navigating the nuances of a first date, find themselves drawn into a meaningful conversation about their hobbies and life experiences.

John: I must say, Emma, I'm really enjoying our talk. It's not often you find someone who shares a passion for hiking and indie music.

Emma: (Smiling) Likewise, John. It's been refreshing to connect on these things. You don't always get the chance on a first date.

As their conversation naturally pauses after discussing their shared interests, Emma decides to break the silence.

Emma: You know, it's interesting how our hobbies often reflect different aspects of our personalities. Like, my love for hiking is all about seeking adventure and embracing challenges. What about you?

John: (Thoughtfully) That's a great point. For me, music is a way to express emotions that words sometimes can't capture. It's like a soundtrack to life, you know?

They dive into a new aspect of their lives, smoothly transitioning from the shared interest of hiking to the deeper meaning behind their respective passions.

- **Smooth Transition:** Emma adeptly transitions the conversation from shared interests to deeper aspects of their personalities, demonstrating a skill in steering discussions.

- **Open-Ended Questioning:** Instead of letting the conversation fizzle out, Emma introduces an open-ended question about the deeper meaning behind their hobbies, encouraging John to share more about himself.

Building Emotional Intelligence

UNDERSTANDING AND EXPRESSING emotions effectively is a vital aspect of emotional intelligence, forming the bedrock of meaningful connections. By accurately identifying and articulating your emotions, you create a foundation for healthier relationships. This involves not just recognizing basic feelings but delving into the nuances that shape your emotional landscape.

Transparent Expression:

Effective emotional expression goes beyond stating feelings; it involves conveying them in a way that fosters understanding. Describing the intensity, triggers, or specific aspects of a situation that evoke certain emotions allows your potential partner to comprehend your emotional world more deeply, promoting empathy and connection.

Being attuned to your emotional responses is invaluable. Instead of merely stating you're excited about a date, expressing the specific aspects that elicit excitement enhances your ability to connect. This emotional granularity also provides your date with valuable insights into what resonates with you.

Recognizing Cues:

Emotional intelligence extends beyond self-awareness to recognizing emotional cues in others. Paying attention to subtle shifts in your date's expressions, body language, and tone of voice during interactions offers glimpses into their emotional state. This allows you to respond with empathy and attunement, deepening the connection.

Impact on Relationships:

The impact of emotional intelligence on relationship building is profound. When both individuals possess a high level of emotional intelligence, conflicts can be navigated with greater understanding and resolution. Expressing emotions effectively and recognizing cues in your partner establish a foundation of trust, contributing to the longevity and depth of the relationship.

Understanding and expressing emotions effectively is the first step in building emotional intelligence. It involves recognizing and articulating your own feelings transparently, being attuned to the emotional cues of others, and fostering a connection that contributes to the longevity and depth of relationships.

RECOGNIZING EMOTIONAL cues in others is a nuanced skill that elevates emotional intelligence, enhancing your ability to forge meaningful connections. In the realm of dating, where non-verbal communication often speaks louder than words, being attuned to your partner's emotional cues is crucial for building rapport and fostering a deeper understanding.

Non-Verbal Communication:

Emotional cues are frequently conveyed through non-verbal channels such as facial expressions, body language, and gestures. A furrowed brow, a subtle smile, or a shift in posture can provide valuable insights into your partner's emotional state. Being observant and interpreting these cues allows you to respond appropriately, demonstrating your attentiveness and empathy.

Active Listening:

Recognizing emotional cues is intertwined with active listening. During conversations, pay close attention not only to the words spoken but also to the emotional undertones. The tone, pitch, and pace of speech can convey emotions that may not be explicitly expressed. Acknowledging these cues demonstrates your sensitivity and genuine interest in understanding your partner.

Empathetic Response:

Responding empathetically to emotional cues creates a supportive and validating dynamic in a relationship. If your partner expresses joy, acknowledging and sharing in that joy strengthens the positive connection. Similarly, if they convey sadness or frustration, responding with empathy and understanding fosters a sense of emotional safety.

Recognizing emotional cues allows you to navigate the intricacies of your partner's feelings. Whether it's gauging their comfort level during a conversation or sensing their enthusiasm about shared interests, this skill enriches the depth of connection and contributes to the overall quality of the dating experience.

AS WE CONCLUDE OUR exploration in Chapter 4: Mastering Conversation Skills, the journey has been a dynamic voyage into the intricacies of effective communication. In the realm of dating, where words carry profound significance, honing conversation skills is paramount

1. **Active Listening Enhances Connection:**

• Techniques for mindful focus and presence in conversations amplify the depth of connections.

• Avoid common pitfalls like interrupting or being mentally elsewhere to truly engage with your date.

1. **Crafting Thoughtful Questions:**

• Encourage meaningful conversations by crafting questions that delve into deeper aspects of life.

• Strive to balance curiosity without prying, respecting the boundaries of the other person.

1. **Sharing Personal Stories:**

• Develop strategies for opening up during conversations, creating a sense of vulnerability.

• Find the right balance between revealing personal aspects and maintaining privacy

1. **Navigating Awkward Silences:**

- Embrace silence as a natural part of conversation, recognizing it as an opportunity for reflection.

- Techniques for gracefully handling pauses can turn moments of potential discomfort into bridges for connection.

1. **Building Emotional Intelligence:**

- Understand and express emotions effectively to foster a deeper connection.

- Recognize emotional cues in others, enhancing your ability to navigate and respond to different emotional states.

In summary, mastering conversation skills involves a delicate interplay of active listening, thoughtful questioning, personal storytelling, and emotional intelligence. By approaching communication with intention and authenticity, you can transform ordinary conversations into meaningful connections, making your dating experience more enriching and fulfilling.

Conquering the Fear of Rejection

Chapter 5

"Rejection is not the end—it's a beginning. Uncover the secrets to facing rejection fear, embracing personal growth, and transforming dating setbacks into stepping stones."

Understanding the Fear of Rejection

REJECTION ANXIETY, a common emotional hurdle in the realm of dating, often originates from various sources. Understanding the roots of this anxiety is crucial for dismantling its power and fostering personal growth.

1. **Past Experiences:**
    a. **Revisiting past instances of rejection provides insight into current anxieties.**
    b. **Unresolved emotions from previous rejections may contribute to heightened anxiety.**

1. **Social Expectations:**
    a. **Societal pressures and expectations regarding relationships play a role.**
    b. **Unrealistic standards and fear of not meeting societal norms can fuel rejection anxiety.**

1. **Self-Perception:**
    a. **Examining one's self-image and perceived worth is essential.**
    b. **Low self-esteem or distorted self-perception may intensify the fear of being rejected.**

1. **Fear of Judgment:**
    a. **The anticipation of judgment from others amplifies rejection anxiety.**
    b. **Unchecked concerns about what others think may hinder authentic self-expression.**

1. **Attachment Style:**

a. Understanding personal attachment styles sheds light on relationship fears.
b. Insecure attachment styles may contribute to heightened sensitivity to rejection.

1. **Cultural Influences:**
    a. **Cultural backgrounds can shape attitudes towards dating and rejection.**
    b. **Awareness of cultural influences aids in contextualizing and addressing anxieties.**

1. **Lack of Self-Compassion:**
    a. **Insufficient self-compassion intensifies the fear of being rejected.**
    b. **Developing self-compassion is a key aspect of mitigating rejection anxiety.**

1. **Unrealistic Perfectionism:**
    a. **Striving for perfection in oneself or potential partners fuels anxiety.**
    b. **Embracing imperfections and realistic expectations reduces rejection-related stress.**

By examining these roots, individuals can gain clarity on the origins of their rejection anxiety, paving the way for targeted strategies to overcome and grow beyond these fears. It's a journey of self-discovery and empowerment, moving from fear to resilience in the face of rejection.

Common Misconceptions about Rejection

NAVIGATING THE LANDSCAPE of rejection is often clouded by misconceptions that can exacerbate fears and hinder personal growth. By debunking these myths, individuals can approach rejection with a clearer perspective and cultivate resilience.

1. Personal Failure:

- **Misconception:** Viewing rejection as a personal failure is a common misunderstanding.
- **Reality:** Rejection often results from compatibility or situational factors, not individual inadequacy.

2. Universal Rejection:

- **Misconception:** Assuming that one rejection means universal unacceptance.
- **Reality:** Rejections are specific to individuals and situations, not indicative of overall worth.

3. Permanent Judgments:

- **Misconception:** Believing that rejection leads to permanent negative judgments.
- **Reality:** People's perceptions can evolve, and one rejection does not define future interactions.

4. Avoidable Pain:

- **Misconception:** Trying to avoid rejection to prevent emotional pain.

- **Reality**: Facing rejection head-on allows for personal growth and resilience over time.

5. Rejection Equals Dislike:

- **Misconception:** Assuming rejection means immediate dislike or disdain.

- **Reality:** Rejection can result from various factors unrelated to personal dislike.

6. Self-Worth Determination:

- **Misconception:** Tying self-worth exclusively to acceptance or rejection.

- **Reality:** Self-worth is multi-faceted and extends beyond individual dating experiences.

7. Rejection as a Reflection:

- **Misconception**: Believing rejection reflects inherent flaws.

- **Reality:** Rejection often mirrors compatibility or differing life paths rather than intrinsic flaws.

8. Singular Narrative:

- **Misconception:** Assuming rejection creates a singular narrative about one's desirability.

- **Reality:** Multiple factors contribute to attraction, and rejection is not a singular verdict.

Disentangling these misconceptions from the experience of rejection is crucial for developing a healthier mindset. By challenging these myths, individuals can approach rejection with resilience, viewing it as a natural part of the dating journey rather than a personal indictment.

THE FEAR OF REJECTION, a powerful and universal emotion, can significantly influence individuals' thoughts, actions, and interpersonal dynamics. Understanding how this fear manifests in behavior is key to overcoming its limitations and fostering personal growth.

1. Self-Sabotage:

- **Behavioral Impact:** Fear of rejection may lead to self-sabotage, where individuals undermine their chances of success to avoid potential rejection.
- **Example:** Declining opportunities for connection or success due to the anticipation of rejection.

2. Avoidance Strategies:

- **Behavioral Impact:** Individuals may adopt avoidance strategies to sidestep situations where rejection is perceived as likely.
- **Example:** Steering clear of social events or refraining from expressing genuine feelings to avoid potential rejection.

3. Approval-Seeking Behavior:

- **Behavioral Impact:** Fear of rejection can fuel a strong desire for approval, influencing behavior to align with perceived expectations.

- **Example:** Modifying opinions or actions to conform to what one believes will be more acceptable.

4. **Overanalyzing and Second-Guessing:**

- **Behavioral Impact:** Fear of rejection can lead to overanalyzing interactions, second-guessing oneself, and seeking constant reassurance.

- **Example:** Ruminating on past conversations, questioning intentions, and seeking validation from others.

5. **Difficulty in Expressing Authenticity:**

- **Behavioral Impact:** A fear of rejection may hinder individuals from expressing their authentic selves, leading to a curated or guarded presentation.

- **Example:** Concealing certain interests or aspects of one's personality to avoid potential disapproval.

6. **Reluctance to Take Initiative:**

- **Behavioral Impact:** Fear of rejection may result in hesitancy to take initiative in social or romantic pursuits.

- **Example:** Avoiding making the first move or initiating conversations due to the fear of negative responses.

7. **Defensiveness and Emotional Guarding:**

- **Behavioral Impact:** Fear of rejection can lead to emotional guarding and defensiveness, protecting oneself from potential emotional pain.

- **Example:** Reacting defensively to constructive feedback or criticism to shield oneself from perceived rejection.

Understanding these behavioral patterns is crucial for individuals looking to navigate the complexities of rejection anxiety. By recognizing the ways in which fear of rejection shapes behavior, individuals can proactively work towards fostering resilience and healthier approaches to interpersonal connections.

Cultivating a Growth Mindset

REJECTION IS A UNIVERSAL experience, a common denominator in the pursuit of success. Rather than viewing rejection as a dead-end, consider it a pivotal stepping stone on your path to personal and professional growth. In this exploration, we delve into the mindset shift needed to embrace rejection, understanding its transformative power, and leveraging it as a tool for continuous improvement.

- **Refuse to be Deterred:** Embracing rejection begins with a fundamental mindset shift. Reject the notion that rejection equates to failure. Understand that setbacks are not a reflection of your worth or capabilities but rather a natural part of the journey toward success. This refusal to be deterred by rejection lays the groundwork for a resilient and growth-oriented mindset.

- **Opportunity in Disguise:** Every rejection is, in essence, an opportunity in disguise. It's not a closed door; it's a redirection toward a more fitting path for your goals. This perspective shift is transformative. Instead of dwelling on what didn't work, focus on the potential for new beginnings and unexplored avenues. Recognizing rejection as a redirection opens the door to innovation and unexpected opportunities.

- **Resilience Building:** Resilience is the ability to bounce back from setbacks stronger than before. Embracing rejection is a profound exercise in resilience building. Each rejection provides an opportunity to reinforce your mental fortitude. Rather than succumbing to disappointment, view rejection as a challenge to overcome. This resilience becomes a powerful asset as you navigate the inevitable challenges on your road to success.

- **Learning and Adapting:** Rejection, when approached with a growth mindset, becomes a rich source of learning. Analyze each rejection objectively. What insights can be gleaned? Treat rejection as feedback, a valuable mechanism for refining your approach. Understanding why a particular path didn't lead to success empowers you to make informed adjustments. This iterative process of learning and adapting positions you for future endeavors with a sharpened strategy.

- **Persistence Pays Off:** Embracing rejection is a testament to your persistence. Success is rarely a linear journey; it often requires multiple attempts and a willingness to face rejection head-on. Each rejection becomes a badge of honor, a marker of your resilience and commitment to your goals. Persistence, coupled with a growth-oriented mindset, transforms rejection from a roadblock into a stepping stone.

- **Cultivating a Growth Mindset:** At its core, embracing rejection is synonymous with cultivating a growth mindset. It is about seeing challenges as opportunities, setbacks as setups for future success. A growth mindset thrives on the belief that abilities can be developed through dedication and hard work. By adopting this perspective, rejection ceases to be a source of discouragement and instead becomes a catalyst for improvement.

Embracing rejection is not a passive acceptance of defeat; it is an active choice to leverage setbacks for personal and professional development. Refuse to be deterred, find the opportunities in disguise, build resilience, learn from experiences, and persist in the face of challenges. This multifaceted approach transforms rejection from a negative force into a positive driver of growth. As you navigate the complex terrain of your goals, remember that embracing rejection is not just a strategy; it's a mindset that propels you toward enduring success.

IN THE PURSUIT OF YOUR goals, rejection is not a roadblock; it's a signpost pointing you toward a better path. Reframing rejection as redirection is a powerful mindset shift that can turn setbacks into stepping stones for success.

1. **Changing the Narrative:**

- Instead of viewing rejection as a closed door, see it as a shift in direction. This is not a denial of your capabilities but an acknowledgment that there might be a more fitting path for your aspirations. Change the narrative from failure to a strategic pivot.

1. **Discovering Alternative Routes:**

- Every rejection opens the door to exploration. Look beyond the immediate setback and identify alternative routes to your goals. This may involve acquiring new skills, seeking different opportunities, or approaching challenges from a fresh perspective. Redirection is about finding a more aligned and fruitful path.

1. **Aligning with Your Purpose:**

- Rejection often nudges you to reassess your goals and values. Use this time for introspection. Is the current trajectory truly aligned with your purpose? Redirection allows you to realign your efforts with your passions and long-term objectives, ensuring a more fulfilling journey.

1. **Embracing Flexibility:**

- Rigidity can be a hindrance to progress. Reframing rejection as redirection requires flexibility. Be open to adapting your plans and embracing change. The ability to pivot gracefully in the face of rejection is a hallmark of resilience and strategic thinking.

1. **Growth through Adaptation:**

- Redirection isn't just about finding a new path; it's about personal and professional growth through adaptation. The skills and insights gained from navigating redirection become invaluable assets in your journey. Each redirection is an opportunity for refinement and improvement.

1. **Building a Robust Mindset:**

- Resilience is the cornerstone of reframing rejection. Redirection is not a concession; it's a strategic move. Cultivate a mindset that sees rejection not as a setback but as a catalyst for growth. This mental fortitude is crucial in maintaining momentum and motivation.

Practical Steps for Redirection:

- **Reflect on Feedback:** Take the time to analyze feedback from rejections. What can you learn? Use this information to adjust your approach and enhance your skills.

- **Identify New Avenues:** Look for alternative paths toward your goals. Are there untapped opportunities or unexplored areas that align with your aspirations?

- **Set Clear Objectives:** Define your objectives clearly. What do you aim to achieve with this redirection? Having a clear vision will guide your efforts in the right direction.

- **Continuous Learning:** Approach redirection as a continuous learning process. Embrace new knowledge and skills that will contribute to your success in the revised trajectory.

Reframing rejection as redirection is a transformative approach to setbacks. It involves changing your perspective, discovering new paths, aligning with your purpose, embracing flexibility, and fostering growth through adaptation. Redirection is not a detour but a strategic move that propels you toward a more fulfilling and successful journey.

REJECTION ISN'T A DEAD end; it's a classroom for invaluable lessons. Here's your roadmap for turning rejection experiences into stepping stones for continuous learning and eventual success.

1. **Objective Analysis:**
   a. **Avoid Emotional Reactivity: When faced with rejection, resist the urge to react emotionally. Instead, take a step back and objectively analyze the situation. Emotional detachment allows for a clearer understanding of the rejection's nuances.**
   b. **Identify Patterns: Look for recurring themes in rejection experiences. Are there commonalities in feedback or reasons for rejection? Identifying patterns helps you pinpoint areas for improvement.**

1. **Feedback as a Compass:**
   a. **Treasure Constructive Criticism: View feedback as a treasure trove of insights. Constructive criticism, though initially uncomfortable, is a guide to refinement. Embrace it with a mindset of improvement rather than defensiveness.**
   b. **Distinguish Between Personal and Professional: Learn to differentiate between personal and professional aspects of feedback. Extract lessons related to your skills and performance while filtering out subjective opinions.**

1. **Adaptation and Skill Enhancement:**
   a. **Adaptability as a Strength: Rejection necessitates adaptation. Use it as an opportunity to hone your adaptability. The ability to adjust your approach based on feedback is a skill that sets you on the**

   path to success.
   b. Continuous Skill Enhancement: Every rejection signals an area for skill enhancement. Identify the skills that need improvement and commit to continuous learning. This proactive approach positions you for future endeavors.

1. Building Resilience:
   a. Resilience Through Reflection: Reflect on the rejection process and acknowledge the associated emotions. This reflective practice contributes to emotional resilience, a key asset in navigating the ups and downs of your journey.
   b. Embrace Setbacks as Setups: Shift your mindset to perceive setbacks as setups for future success. Each rejection is a chapter in your story, contributing to the narrative of growth and resilience.

1. Strategic Planning for the Future:
   a. Strategize Based on Insights: Use the insights gained from rejection experiences to formulate a strategic plan for the future. How can you adjust your approach? What new strategies can you implement to increase your chances of success?
   b. Set Realistic Goals: Reevaluate and set realistic goals. Align your objectives with the lessons learned, ensuring that your aspirations are both ambitious and attainable.

Practical Implementation:

- **Create a Rejection Journal:** Maintain a rejection journal to document experiences, emotions, and key takeaways. Regularly revisit it for insights and to track your progress.

- **Seek Mentorship:** Engage with mentors who can provide guidance based on their own rejection experiences. Their perspectives can offer valuable insights and encouragement.

- **Celebrate Small Wins:** Acknowledge and celebrate small victories resulting from the lessons learned. This positive reinforcement reinforces the idea that rejection is a catalyst for growth.

- **Network for Insights:** Connect with individuals in your field to gain diverse insights. Networking not only expands your knowledge base but also provides a support system during challenging times.

Learning from rejection experiences is a proactive approach to personal and professional growth. Through objective analysis, feedback utilization, skill enhancement, resilience building, and strategic planning, rejection becomes a teacher rather than an obstacle. Embrace rejection as a part of your learning journey, and let it propel you toward future successes.

Building Resilience

TRANSFORMING MINDSET:

- Rejection isn't a dead end but a temporary detour. Shift your perspective; view it as a momentary setback rather than a reflection of your abilities. Develop a growth-focused mindset, considering each rejection as an opportunity for personal and professional advancement.

Coping Strategies:

- After a rejection, engage in self-reflection without dwelling in negativity. Objectively analyze the situation to extract valuable insights. Employ healthy coping mechanisms like exercise or meditation to maintain mental well-being.

Learning from Rejection:

- Consider rejection as feedback, a guide for improvement. Identify patterns and areas for adaptation. Embrace flexibility; let rejections be opportunities to refine your strategies and enhance resilience.

Building Support Networks:

- Connect with friends, mentors, or support groups for emotional reinforcement. Share experiences and seek guidance from mentors who have navigated rejections. Emotional support is a powerful ally in building resilience.

Maintaining Perspective:

- Keep your long-term goals in focus; rejections are transient hurdles, not the conclusion of your journey. Celebrate progress, acknowledging growth through incremental victories and the resilience cultivated from rejection experiences.

Practical Application:

- **Insightful Journaling:** Create a rejection journal for concise documentation. Regular reflection enhances self-awareness and resilience.

- **Mindfulness Practices:** Incorporate mindfulness techniques into your routine. Stay present and grounded during challenging times.

- **Continuous Learning Commitment:** Embrace rejection as an avenue for learning. Pursue opportunities for personal and professional development, leveraging setbacks as catalysts for improvement.

Embrace rejection as a strategic challenge, not a roadblock. Transform your mindset, employ coping strategies, learn from experiences, foster support networks, and maintain a long-term perspective. Let resilience guide you, turning setbacks into stepping stones on your journey to success.

In the face of disappointment, adopting strategic strategies is crucial for a resilient rebound.

Acknowledging Emotions:

- Disappointment is a natural emotion. Allow yourself to acknowledge and embrace it without judgment. This acknowledgment is the first step toward a thoughtful recovery.

Constructive Coping:

- Engage in activities that bring joy or relaxation, providing a healthy outlet for your emotions. Whether it's a walk, a hobby, or time with loved ones, these activities can ease the immediate impact of disappointment. Simultaneously, avoid falling into the trap of endless rumination. Instead, focus on actionable steps to move forward.

Reframing the Narrative:

- Actively seek silver linings within the disappointment. Embrace a learning mindset, extracting valuable lessons from the experience. Consider it a platform for personal and professional growth, where challenges become opportunities.

Strategic Action:

- Reassess your goals in the wake of disappointment. Are they still aligned with your aspirations? Redefine objectives based on the insights gained. Develop a concrete plan with actionable steps to overcome the disappointment—a roadmap guiding you toward regaining momentum.

Building Resilience:

- Frame disappointment as a hurdle, not a roadblock. Resilience thrives when challenges are faced with determination. Keep your long-term goals in mind. Shift your focus from short-term setbacks to the overarching objectives you strive to achieve.

Bouncing back from disappointment requires acknowledging emotions, employing constructive coping mechanisms, reframing the narrative positively, taking strategic action, and building resilience. Use disappointment as a catalyst for growth, learning, and propelling yourself toward your long-term objectives.

CULTIVATING A POSITIVE mindset is not just an aspiration but a strategic choice that can significantly impact your well-being and success. It's about more than just seeing the glass half full; it's a mindset that empowers you to navigate challenges, embrace opportunities, and foster resilience in the face of adversity.

Why cultivate a positive mindset? Because the lens through which you view the world shapes your experiences and responses. A positive mindset is not about denying the existence of difficulties but about choosing to approach them with optimism and a belief in your ability to overcome. It's a self-fulfilling prophecy; what you focus on expands, and a positive mindset lays the foundation for growth, both personally and professionally.

You encounter a setback at work. A project you invested time in doesn't yield the expected results. In the face of this disappointment, a positive mindset reframes the situation. Rather than dwelling on failure, you see it as a learning opportunity. You extract lessons, identify areas for improvement, and pivot your approach. This positive outlook not only positions you for future success but also fosters a resilient spirit that can weather future challenges.

Why cultivate a positive mindset?

- **Enhanced Resilience:** Positivity cultivates resilience, allowing you to bounce back from setbacks with newfound strength.

- **Improved Problem-Solving:** A positive mindset encourages a solution-focused approach, leading to more effective problem-solving.

- **Health Benefits:** Studies show that a positive mindset is linked to lower stress levels, improved immune function, and overall better health.

In a demanding work environment, individuals with a positive mindset are more likely to view challenges as opportunities for growth. Instead of succumbing to stress, they see pressure as a chance to showcase their abilities and develop new skills. This mindset not only enhances their performance but also contributes to a healthier work-life balance.

Now, let's delve into the practical aspects of cultivating a positive mindset.

1. Gratitude Practice:

- Expressing gratitude is a powerful tool for fostering positivity. Regularly reflect on the things you are thankful for, whether big or small. This practice shifts your focus from what's lacking to the abundance in your life.

2. Positive Affirmations:

- Integrate positive affirmations into your daily routine. Affirmations like "I am capable," or "I embrace challenges as opportunities" can reshape your self-perception and reinforce a positive mindset.

3. Surround Yourself with Positivity:

- Evaluate your environment and relationships. Surround yourself with positive influences that uplift and inspire. Limit exposure to negativity, whether in the media or toxic relationships, to maintain a constructive outlook.

4. Learn and Adapt:

- A positive mindset involves seeing setbacks as stepping stones, not roadblocks. Embrace a mindset of continuous learning and adaptation. View challenges as opportunities to acquire new skills and refine existing ones.

Cultivating a positive mindset is not a one-time effort but a continuous journey. It's a commitment to shaping your thoughts, responses, and ultimately, your reality. As you integrate these practices into your daily life, you'll find that positivity becomes a habit—one that propels you toward greater fulfillment and success. Remember, in the tapestry of life, a positive mindset is the thread that weaves a resilient and optimistic narrative.

Setting Realistic Expectations

THE FEAR OF REJECTION often finds its roots in the expectations we carry. These expectations act as silent architects, constructing intricate scenarios in our minds that, when unmet, fuel the fear of rejection. Understanding the pivotal role expectations play in this fear is the first step towards building resilience in the face of romantic uncertainties.

The Weight of Unrealistic Expectations:

Expectations, when left unchecked, can morph into unrealistic fantasies. The anticipation of a flawless interaction, a perfect date, or instant connection can elevate anxiety. The higher the expectations, the more profound the fear of falling short. It's essential to recognize that perfection is an unrealistic standard, and dating is a nuanced journey filled with uncertainties.

Comparisons Amplifying Anxiety:

Social comparisons exacerbate the fear of rejection. When expectations are based on idealized notions or comparisons with others, the fear intensifies. The perception that others effortlessly navigate the dating landscape can lead to self-doubt. Unmet expectations in such scenarios can trigger anxiety about not measuring up, compounding the fear of rejection.

Consider a scenario where the expectation is an instantaneous and profound connection on the first date. If this expectation is not met, it can lead to disappointment and self-doubt, fueling the fear of rejection. Understanding that genuine connections take time and unfold organically can help recalibrate expectations, mitigating the fear associated with unrealized anticipations.

Strategies for Setting Realistic Dating Expectations:

1. **Embrace Realism Over Perfection:**

• Shift focus from perfection to authenticity. Embrace the idea that meaningful connections are built on genuine interactions rather than flawless scenarios.

1. **Be Mindful of Social Comparisons:**

• Recognize that everyone's dating journey is unique. Avoid comparing your experiences to others, as it often leads to unrealistic expectations. Your path is yours alone.

1. **Communicate Openly:**

• Prioritize open communication. Clearly express your intentions and expectations with your dating partner. Mutual understanding ensures alignment and reduces the likelihood of unmet expectations.

1. **Learn from Each Interaction:**

- Treat each interaction as a learning experience. Rather than expecting a predetermined outcome, focus on gaining insights about yourself and your compatibility with the other person.

How Adjusting Expectations Enhances Resilience:

- **Reduced Vulnerability to Setbacks:** Realistic expectations act as a buffer against setbacks. When expectations are grounded, the impact of unmet anticipations is less severe, fostering resilience.

- **Enhanced Adaptability:** Adjusting expectations enhances adaptability. Instead of fixating on a specific outcome, individuals with realistic expectations are more adaptable to the nuances of the dating journey.

- **Improved Self-Image:** Realistic expectations contribute to a healthier self-image. Acknowledging that no one is flawless and that connections take time fosters self-acceptance and diminishes the fear of rejection.

Understanding the role of expectations in the fear of rejection is pivotal. By embracing realism, avoiding social comparisons, and communicating openly, individuals can set realistic dating expectations. Adjusting these expectations not only enhances resilience but also fosters a more positive and authentic approach to the complexities of romantic relationships.

SETTING REALISTIC DATING expectations is a key ingredient for navigating the complexities of romance with resilience and authenticity. Rather than succumbing to the pressures of unrealistic ideals, employing strategic approaches can lead to more fulfilling and grounded connections.

1. **Embrace Individuality:**

- **Why:** Each person brings a unique set of experiences, values, and expectations to the table. Embracing individuality allows you to appreciate the diversity in the dating landscape.

- **Example:** Instead of expecting universal dating norms, recognize that what works for one person may not work for another. Embrace the beauty of diverse perspectives.

1. **Focus on Connection, Not Perfection:**

- **Why:** Perfection is an elusive standard that often leads to disappointment. Shifting the focus from achieving perfection to fostering genuine connections paves the way for more authentic and meaningful relationships.

- **Example:** Instead of expecting flawless interactions, focus on getting to know your date and building a connection over shared interests and values.

1. **Set Intentions, Not Outcomes:**

- **Why:** While it's natural to desire positive outcomes, fixating on specific results can lead to undue pressure and anxiety. Setting intentions allows for a more flexible and adaptive approach to dating.

- **Example:** Rather than expecting a relationship to progress at a predetermined pace, set intentions to enjoy the journey, learn about yourself and your partner, and see where it leads.

1. **Open Communication:**

- **Why:** Transparent communication is the cornerstone of healthy relationships. Clearly expressing your intentions, desires, and boundaries fosters mutual understanding and aligns expectations.

- **Example:** Communicate openly about your expectations regarding commitment, exclusivity, and the pace of the relationship. This avoids misunderstandings and promotes a shared vision.

1. **Learn from Each Experience:**

- **Why:** Dating is a dynamic learning process. Each interaction offers insights into your preferences, deal-breakers, and the qualities you value in a partner.

- **Example:** Treat every date as an opportunity to learn about yourself and others. Adjust your expectations based on the lessons gained, contributing to a more refined and realistic approach.

- **Individuality**: Embrace diverse perspectives and values.

- **Connection Over Perfection:** Focus on building genuine connections.

- **Intentions, Not Outcomes:** Set intentions for the journey, not predetermined outcomes.

- **Open Communication:** Clearly express intentions, desires, and boundaries.

- **Learn and Adapt:** Treat each experience as a learning opportunity.

By integrating these strategies into your dating mindset, you foster an environment conducive to realistic expectations. Embracing individuality, prioritizing connection, setting intentions, promoting open communication, and learning from each experience contribute to a more grounded and resilient approach to dating. Remember, the journey is as important as the destination, and realistic expectations pave the way for more satisfying and enduring connections.

ADJUSTING EXPECTATIONS is a powerful tool in cultivating resilience within the realm of dating. By embracing a more flexible and realistic mindset, individuals can navigate the uncertainties and challenges of romantic relationships with greater adaptability and emotional strength.

1. **Reduced Vulnerability to Setbacks:**

- **Why:** Realistic expectations act as a buffer against setbacks. When expectations are grounded, the impact of unmet anticipations is less severe.

- **Example:** If a date doesn't unfold as expected, someone with adjusted expectations is more likely to view it as a minor deviation rather than a significant failure, reducing vulnerability to emotional setbacks.

1. **Enhanced Adaptability:**

- **Why:** Adjusting expectations fosters adaptability. Rather than rigidly adhering to a predefined script, individuals with flexible expectations can navigate the twists and turns of the dating journey more gracefully.

- **Example:** If a relationship takes an unexpected turn, someone with adjusted expectations is more likely to adapt, pivot, and find constructive solutions rather than becoming overwhelmed.

1. **Improved Self-Image:**

- **Why:** Realistic expectations contribute to a healthier self-image. Acknowledging that no one is flawless and that connections take time fosters self-acceptance.

- **Example:** If a relationship doesn't progress as quickly as anticipated, someone with adjusted expectations is more likely to view it as a natural part of the process rather than a personal shortcoming, leading to improved self-esteem.

1. **Strengthened Emotional Resilience:**

- **Why:** Embracing adjusted expectations nurtures emotional resilience. Individuals are better equipped to bounce back from disappointments and setbacks, viewing them as integral parts of the learning and growth process.

- **Example:** If a romantic interest doesn't reciprocate feelings, someone with adjusted expectations sees it as an opportunity to learn about compatibility and personal preferences, strengthening emotional resilience.

1. **Promotion of a Growth Mindset:**

- **Why:** Adjusting expectations aligns with a growth mindset. It encourages individuals to view challenges as opportunities for learning and personal development.

- **Example:** If a date provides constructive feedback or highlights areas for improvement, someone with adjusted expectations sees it as valuable input for personal growth rather than a critique.

- **Reduced Vulnerability:** Grounded expectations lessen the impact of setbacks.

- **Enhanced Adaptability:** Adjusted expectations foster flexibility in navigating challenges.

- **Improved Self-Image:** Realistic expectations contribute to healthier self-acceptance.

- **Strengthened Resilience:** Embracing setbacks as learning opportunities enhances emotional resilience.

- **Growth Mindset:** Adjusted expectations align with viewing challenges as avenues for personal development.

Adjusting expectations enhances resilience by reducing vulnerability to setbacks, promoting adaptability, improving self-image, strengthening emotional resilience, and nurturing a growth mindset. By embracing a mindset that acknowledges the fluid and unpredictable nature of dating, individuals can approach romantic relationships with greater fortitude and a positive outlook on personal growth and connection.

Moving Forward After Rejection

EXPERIENCING REJECTION in the realm of dating can be disheartening, but it's crucial to recognize that rejection doesn't define your worth. Instead of internalizing it as a personal failure, view it as a redirection toward a more suitable match. This mindset shift is the first step in regaining confidence, acknowledging that rejection is often about compatibility rather than inadequacy.

1. **Reflect and Reframe:**

• **Why:** Reflection is key to understanding the dynamics of rejection. Take a moment to reflect on the experience without dwelling on perceived shortcomings. Reframe it as an opportunity for self-discovery and redirection.

• **Example:** If compatibility factors didn't align, see it as a valuable redirection toward a more harmonious connection.

1. **Highlight Your Strengths:**

• **Why:** Reminding yourself of your strengths is a powerful confidence booster. Focus on the positive qualities that make you unique and valuable.

• **Example:** Create a list of your accomplishments, attributes, and positive feedback. This reinforces a positive self-image and aids in rebuilding confidence.

1. **Seek Support and Encouragement:**

- **Why:** Reaching out to a support network provides valuable encouragement and perspective. Surrounding yourself with positive influences can counteract the emotional impact of rejection.

- **Example:** Share your experience with friends or family who can offer insights and encouragement, fostering a renewed sense of confidence.

1. **Set Realistic Goals:**

- **Why:** Establishing realistic and achievable goals is crucial for rebuilding confidence gradually. Celebrate small victories along the way to regain a sense of accomplishment.

- **Example:** Instead of aiming for immediate success in dating, set goals like initiating casual conversations or exploring new social activities. These small steps contribute to gradual confidence rebuilding.

1. **Focus on Self-Improvement:**

- **Why:** Using rejection as motivation for self-improvement is empowering. Channeling energy into personal growth, whether through learning new skills or enhancing well-being, naturally boosts confidence.

- **Example:** Enroll in a class, start a fitness routine, or explore activities aligned with your interests. This proactive approach contributes to self-improvement and increased confidence.

1. **Challenge Negative Thoughts:**

- **Why:** Identifying and challenging negative thoughts stemming from rejection is essential. Replace self-critical thoughts with more balanced and empowering perspectives.

- **Example:** If thoughts like "I'm not good enough" arise, counteract them with affirmations such as "I am deserving of love and respect." This reshaping of thoughts contributes to a more positive self-view.

Rebuilding confidence post-rejection is a process rooted in reflection, positive reinforcement, and personal growth. By adopting these strategies, you not only recover from rejection but also emerge with increased self-assurance, ready to approach future relationships with optimism and resilience.

Unveiling the Lessons:

Rejection need not be a dead-end; rather, it can be a turning point for growth. What lessons can be extracted from rejection experiences? It's an opportunity to delve into the dynamics of communication, personal preferences, and areas for self-improvement.

Unpacking Personal Preferences:

Why did the rejection occur? Examining your own preferences and those of the other party unveils valuable insights. Were there misalignments in values, expectations, or communication styles? By understanding these nuances, rejection becomes a guide to refining your understanding of what truly matters to you.

Reflecting for Growth:

Rejection prompts a journey of self-reflection. What aspects of the interaction could be enhanced? Whether it's communication skills, setting clear expectations, or managing emotions, each rejection holds a mirror to areas for personal development.

Refining Communication:

Take rejection as a lesson in communication. Were expectations effectively communicated? Did both parties understand each other's intentions? Using rejection as a catalyst for refining communication skills ensures clearer connections in future interactions.

Navigating Future Relationships:

Rejection experiences, when dissected for lessons, become invaluable guides for navigating future relationships. Imagine a rejection not as a closed door, but as a directional sign pointing towards a path of improved understanding, better communication, and enhanced self-awareness.

In essence, turning rejection into valuable lessons is a reflective journey—one that transforms setbacks into stepping stones for personal and relational growth.

WHY APPROACH FUTURE dating with renewed optimism?

Future dating holds the promise of new connections, experiences, and opportunities for personal growth. Approaching it with renewed optimism sets the stage for a positive mindset, enhancing your ability to navigate the complexities of relationships.

How does optimism shape your dating experience?

Optimism acts as a powerful lens, allowing you to see challenges as opportunities and setbacks as lessons. It instills confidence, resilience, and a belief that each interaction contributes to your journey, whether it leads to a lasting connection or valuable self-discovery.

Consider a past dating disappointment. Instead of letting it cast a shadow on future endeavors, approach it with a mindset of optimism. View it as a redirection toward a more compatible match or a lesson in refining your preferences. Optimism becomes the driving force that transforms setbacks into stepping stones for a more fulfilling dating experience.

- **Embrace New Opportunities:** Future dating opens doors to new connections and experiences.
- **Optimism as a Mindset:** Approach dating with optimism for a positive and resilient mindset.
- **See Challenges as Opportunities:** Optimism transforms challenges into opportunities for growth.
- **Belief in Your Journey:** Each interaction, whether successful or not, contributes to your unique dating journey.
- Redirection and Lessons: Optimism turns setbacks into redirections toward compatibility or valuable lessons.

Approaching future dating with renewed optimism shapes your mindset, allowing you to embrace opportunities, see challenges as growth experiences, and believe in the unique journey each interaction contributes to.

Key highlights

- **Understanding the Fear:** We explored the roots of rejection anxiety, debunked common misconceptions, and dissected how the fear of rejection profoundly influences behavior.

- **Cultivating Growth:** A pivotal shift in mindset was introduced, advocating the embracement of rejection as a catalyst for personal growth. This involves reframing rejection as redirection and extracting valuable lessons from these experiences.

- **Building Resilience:** The chapter outlined strategies for developing resilience, including bouncing back from disappointments and fostering a positive mindset. Resilience became the cornerstone of facing rejection with strength and fortitude.

- **Realistic Expectations:** We delved into the role of expectations in the fear of rejection and provided practical strategies for setting realistic dating expectations. Adjusting these expectations emerged as a powerful tool in enhancing resilience.

- **Moving Forward:** The chapter concluded by offering actionable strategies for regaining confidence post-rejection, turning rejection experiences into valuable lessons, and approaching future dating with a renewed sense of optimism.

CONQUERING THE FEAR of rejection is not just about avoiding it but navigating it with resilience and optimism. By understanding its roots, fostering a growth mindset, and building resilience, one can turn rejections into opportunities for personal development and approach future dating with newfound confidence.

Creating Intimate Connections

Chapter 6

"As the poet Rumi once said, 'The wound is the place where the light enters you.' In the realm of relationships, what wounds can teach us about creating connections that withstand the trials of time?"

The Importance of Emotional Intimacy

LET'S DELVE INTO A crucial aspect of relationships: understanding the distinction between physical and emotional intimacy.

Physical Intimacy:

In the realm of connection, physical intimacy encompasses the tangible expressions – the hugs, kisses, and shared moments. It's the visible part of the bond, the warmth you can feel.

Emotional Intimacy:

Now, emotional intimacy is where the real depth resides. It involves opening up, sharing feelings, thoughts, and vulnerabilities. It's the invisible, powerful force that forges a profound connection beyond the surface.

Why It Matters:

Recognizing this difference is essential. While physical closeness is delightful, it's the emotional connection that elevates a relationship into something enduring and special. It's the secret ingredient.

Imagine a cozy night with someone special. The physical closeness is there, but what truly makes it memorable is the laughter, the genuine talks, and that feeling of genuine understanding.

- **Balancing Acts:** Physical and emotional intimacy are like the yin and yang of relationships – both essential for a harmonious connection.

- **Depth Appreciation:** Understanding this difference allows us to appreciate the necessity of connecting not just on a visible level but from the heart.

- **Harmonious Blend:** The most fulfilling connections are a perfect blend of the tangible and the emotional.

So, let's acknowledge the dance between physical and emotional intimacy, enriching our connections and creating bonds that are not just seen but deeply felt. Cheers to building those meaningful connections!

Emotional intimacy acts as the secret sauce, elevating connections from the ordinary to the extraordinary. Let's delve into how this profound aspect fosters deeper, more meaningful bonds.

---

1. **Shared Vulnerability:**

Opening up and being vulnerable forms the bedrock of emotional intimacy. It's about laying bare your fears, dreams, and insecurities, creating a space for authentic connection.

- **Mutual Openness:** Both partners sharing their innermost thoughts and emotions creates an environment of trust and authenticity.

PICTURE A COUPLE FACING a significant life decision. By openly discussing their fears and uncertainties, they deepen their connection and collaboratively navigate challenges.

1. **Building Trust:**

Trust is the currency of any relationship, and emotional intimacy is the cornerstone in its construction. Sharing inner thoughts and feelings establishes a foundation of trust.

- **Foundation of Trust:** Vulnerability and openness create a bond built on mutual respect and understanding, forming the basis of trust.

Revealing personal experiences and receiving a non-judgmental, empathetic response strengthens the trust between partners.

1. **Enhancing Emotional Connection:**

Emotional intimacy heightens the emotional connection, making partners attuned to each other's needs and fostering a deeper understanding.

- **Attunement to Emotions:** Partners become sensitive to joys, sorrows, and nuances, deepening the emotional connection.

When a partner senses your mood without words and responds with care, it demonstrates an enhanced emotional connection.

In essence, emotional intimacy is the glue that binds relationships, creating an environment where individuals feel seen, heard, and truly understood. It's the catalyst for forging connections that go beyond the surface, enriching each other's lives in profound and lasting ways.

NURTURING EMOTIONAL intimacy is akin to cultivating a rare and beautiful flower. It requires attention, care, and a deep understanding of each other's emotional landscapes. Let's explore how to foster this crucial element in the dating journey.

1. **Prioritize Open Communication:**

Clear and open communication is the soil in which emotional intimacy thrives. It involves not only expressing your thoughts but also actively listening to your partner.

- **Expressing Thoughts:** Share your feelings, desires, and even uncertainties. Being open creates an environment conducive to emotional connection.

- **Active Listening:** Actively engage in conversations, demonstrating a genuine interest in your partner's emotions and perspectives.

Imagine discussing future aspirations. Instead of generalities, openly share your dreams and fears. Your partner reciprocates by actively listening, fostering a deeper understanding of each other's emotional landscapes.

1. **Create Shared Experiences:**

Shared experiences create a bond that goes beyond the surface. Engaging in activities together builds a reservoir of memories that contribute to emotional intimacy.

- **Meaningful Activities:** Choose activities that resonate with both of you. Whether it's cooking together or embarking on a weekend adventure, shared experiences strengthen the emotional connection.

- **Building Memories:** Meaningful moments create a shared history, enhancing the emotional fabric of your relationship.

Participating in a cooking class together not only provides a fun activity but also allows you to navigate challenges as a team, deepening your emotional connection.

1. **Be Authentic and Vulnerable:**

Authenticity and vulnerability are the sunlight that nourishes emotional intimacy. Allow yourselves to be seen for who you truly are, flaws and all.

- **Authentic Expression:** Be genuine in expressing your thoughts and feelings. Authenticity builds trust and a sense of connection.

- **Embrace Vulnerability:** Share aspects of yourself that may feel vulnerable. This openness creates an atmosphere of trust and mutual understanding.

Sharing a personal story about overcoming a challenge demonstrates authenticity and vulnerability. Your partner reciprocates, creating a space for a more profound emotional connection.

1. **Cultivate Emotional Awareness:**

Emotional intimacy is rooted in an understanding of each other's emotional needs. Cultivate awareness of your partner's feelings and respond with empathy.

- **Recognize Emotional Cues:** Pay attention to subtle cues that reveal your partner's emotional state. This heightened awareness deepens emotional connections.

- **Empathetic Responses:** Respond to your partner's emotions with empathy. Acknowledge and validate their feelings, fostering a sense of emotional security.

If your partner expresses excitement about a personal achievement, recognizing their joy and celebrating together demonstrates emotional awareness and connection.

Nurturing emotional intimacy requires deliberate effort and intention. By prioritizing open communication, creating shared experiences, embracing authenticity and vulnerability, and cultivating emotional awareness, you lay the foundation for a dating journey rich in emotional connection and depth.

Building Trust Gradually

BUILDING A STRONG FOUNDATION in any relationship starts with trust. Trust is the invisible thread that weaves through the fabric of intimate connections, holding them together and allowing them to flourish. As you navigate the complexities of building a meaningful relationship, understanding the pivotal role of trust is paramount.

Why Trust Matters:

Trust forms the bedrock of emotional intimacy, creating a sense of security and openness between partners. It goes beyond mere reliability; trust is about vulnerability and confidence in each other. Without trust, true intimacy becomes elusive.

Strategies for Building Trust Over Time:

1. **Consistency is Key:**

- Demonstrating reliability through consistent actions builds a sense of predictability.

- Small, reliable gestures over time contribute significantly to trust.

1. **Open Communication and Transparency:**

• Foster an environment where open communication is valued.

• Transparent discussions about feelings, expectations, and concerns build trust.

1. **Shared Experiences and Memories:**

• Creating shared positive experiences fosters a sense of unity.

• Shared memories serve as a testament to the strength of your connection.

Recognizing and Addressing Trust Issues:

1. **Acknowledge and Communicate:**

• Recognize when trust issues arise and address them promptly.

• Open, non-confrontational communication is essential in resolving concerns.

1. **Understanding the Root Cause:**

• Dig deeper to understand the underlying causes of trust issues.

• Addressing root issues ensures a more comprehensive resolution.

1. **Rebuilding Trust Through Actions:**

- Actions speak louder than words. Consistently demonstrating trustworthiness is crucial.

- Be patient, as rebuilding trust is a gradual process that requires commitment.

Trust acts as the compass, guiding you through the twists and turns of a relationship. Embrace it, nurture it, and watch as the bonds of your connection strengthen over time. Remember, trust is not just given; it's earned through shared experiences, open communication, and a commitment to building something lasting together.

TRUST, THE BEDROCK of strong relationships, is nurtured through deliberate actions and consistent efforts. Whether you're forging a new connection or reinforcing an existing one, these practical strategies will guide you in building trust over time.

---

1. **Consistent Reliability:**

- *Build confidence through consistency. Deliver on commitments and be reliably present.*

- Consistent small actions lay the foundation for enduring trust.

1. **Open Communication:**

- *Foster trust through transparency. Encourage open dialogues about expectations and concerns.*

- Address issues promptly and honestly to prevent misunderstandings.

1. **Shared Positive Experiences:**

- *Forge unity through shared memories. Engage in activities that create lasting connections.*

- Positive shared experiences contribute to the tapestry of trust.

1. **Vulnerability and Honesty:**

- *Cultivate trust with openness. Share thoughts and feelings authentically.*

- Honesty, even in challenging moments, establishes an authentic connection.

1. **Setting and Respecting Boundaries:**

- *Establish and uphold clear boundaries. Communicate and respect personal limits.*

- Consistent boundary adherence reinforces mutual trust.

1. **Reliable Decision-Making:**

- *Build confidence with sound judgment. Align decisions with shared values.*

- Demonstrating reliability in choices reinforces trust.

1. **Dependability in Tough Times:**

• *Show loyalty during challenges. Be a reliable partner in navigating difficulties.*

• Weathering storms together strengthens the foundation of trust.

1. **Accountability for Mistakes:**

• *Demonstrate integrity through ownership. Acknowledge and rectify mistakes.*

• Taking responsibility fosters trust in your commitment to growth.

1. **Consistent Positive Affirmations:**

• *Nurture trust with appreciation. Offer genuine compliments and affirmations regularly.*

• Positive reinforcement contributes to a trust-enriched atmosphere.

1. **Time and Patience:**

• *Allow trust to unfold naturally. Patience is key to the organic development of trust.*

• Cultivate a relationship that stands the test of time through gradual, genuine investment.

INCORPORATE THESE STRATEGIES into your relationship journey, weaving a tapestry of trust that strengthens with each shared experience and intentional action.

NAVIGATING TRUST ISSUES in Relationships

Trust is the bedrock of any thriving relationship, but sometimes, challenges arise that test its foundation. Recognizing and addressing trust issues is an essential aspect of fostering a resilient and enduring connection. In this exploration, we'll navigate the complexities of trust issues, understanding their dynamics and offering insights for resolution.

Understanding the Dynamics:

Trust issues in relationships can manifest in various ways, often with subtle cues that may go unnoticed. Persistent doubts, a reluctance to be vulnerable, or a sense of insecurity can signal the presence of trust issues. It's essential to grasp the intricate dynamics of how these issues surface and impact the overall connection between partners.

Common Signs of Trust Issues:

Identifying trust issues requires a keen awareness of common signs. These may include a hesitancy to fully open up, doubts about your partner's intentions, or a persistent fear of betrayal. By recognizing these signs early on, individuals can take proactive steps to address and alleviate trust-related concerns.

Root Causes of Trust Issues:

Delving into the root causes of trust issues unveils a complex landscape. Past betrayals, whether in previous relationships or personal experiences, often contribute to the development of trust issues. Insecurities about self-worth, fear of vulnerability, or unresolved conflicts may further deepen these challenges. Understanding these underlying causes is crucial for effective resolution.

Interactive Self-Assessment:

To enhance self-awareness, we provide an interactive self-assessment tool. This tool encourages reflection on personal experiences and feelings, empowering individuals to identify and acknowledge potential trust issues within themselves or their relationships. Self-awareness becomes a catalyst for proactive steps toward resolution.

Navigating trust issues is a journey that requires patience, understanding, and a commitment to growth. By recognizing the signs, understanding the dynamics, and addressing the root causes, individuals can pave the way for a healthier, more trusting relationship.

Shared Values and Goals

IN THE INTRICATE DANCE of relationships, understanding and aligning core values form the bedrock of a strong and lasting connection. Here, we explore the crucial process of identifying and discussing core values, illuminating the path toward deeper understanding and harmony in relationships.

1. The Significance of Core Values:

- Core values are the fundamental beliefs and principles that shape who we are.
- Identifying and understanding these values is pivotal for fostering genuine connections.

2. The Role of Core Values in Relationships:

- Core values act as guiding principles, influencing decision-making and priorities.
- In relationships, shared core values contribute to a sense of unity and purpose.

3. Identifying Your Core Values:

- Reflect on your beliefs, priorities, and non-negotiables.
- Pinpoint the values that are integral to your identity and worldview.

4. Discussing Core Values with Your Partner:

- Initiate open and honest conversations about your respective core values.
- Share personal insights and experiences that shaped your value system.

5. Navigating Differences in Core Values:

- Acknowledge that differences may exist and that's okay.
- Discuss and find common ground, focusing on understanding and respect.

6. The Evolution of Core Values:

- Recognize that core values can evolve over time.
- Regularly revisit and discuss your values to ensure alignment as your relationship grows.

7. Strengthening Connection Through Shared Values:

- Identify areas where your core values align and reinforce your connection.
- Leverage shared values to build a foundation of trust and understanding.

8.Building a Life Together:

- Aligning life goals with shared core values enhances compatibility.

- Collaboratively create a vision for the future that reflects your shared values.

Navigating the terrain of core values requires openness, communication, and a willingness to understand both yourself and your partner. By identifying, discussing, and aligning core values, you lay the groundwork for a relationship that not only survives but thrives on the strength of shared beliefs and mutual understanding.

SHARED GOALS EMERGE as a potent force that unites individuals with a common purpose. They act as a beacon, providing a shared vision that aligns the aspirations of partners. The significance lies not only in the destination but in the journey taken together.

- Initiate open conversations about individual aspirations and dreams.

- Collaboratively set achievable yet meaningful objectives that resonate with both partners.

Shared Goals as a Unifying Force:

Embarking on the journey of building shared goals requires openness and active communication. Initiate conversations about your individual aspirations and dreams. Share your visions for the future, and actively listen to your partner's aspirations. This open dialogue creates a foundation for identifying common ground. Collaboratively set achievable yet meaningful objectives that resonate with both partners. These goals should reflect shared values and contribute to the growth and fulfillment of each individual while aligning with the shared vision for the relationship.

Establishing Common Ground:

Shared goals play a pivotal role in establishing common ground within a relationship. They serve as a bridge that connects partners on a deeper level, providing a shared space where their individual journeys intersect.

- Engage in open and honest discussions about individual values and long-term aspirations.

- Establish shared goals that resonate with both partners, ensuring they reflect a collective vision for the relationship.

Building shared goals involves more than just setting objectives; it's about establishing common ground that creates a foundation for understanding and collaboration. Engage in open and honest discussions about individual values and long-term aspirations. Actively listen to your partner's perspective and seek to understand their core values. Look for commonalities and areas where your dreams align. Establish shared goals that resonate with both partners, ensuring they reflect a collective vision for the relationship. These goals should create a sense of unity and purpose, serving as a driving force for the journey you embark on together.

Creating a Sense of Partnership:

Pursuing shared goals within a relationship fosters a profound sense of partnership. It transforms the journey of achieving objectives into a joint effort, where both individuals actively contribute to the shared vision.

- Choose goals that require collaboration and mutual effort.

- Celebrate achievements as a team, reinforcing the sense of partnership in reaching shared goals.

Creating a sense of partnership involves actively working together towards shared objectives. Choose goals that necessitate collaboration and mutual effort. Whether it's planning a future together, building a home, or pursuing individual and shared career goals, ensure that both partners actively contribute to the journey. Establish clear roles and responsibilities for each partner in the pursuit of shared objectives. This clarity promotes a sense of accountability and ensures that both individuals are invested in the shared goals. Celebrating achievements as a team marks significant milestones in the journey of your relationship, reinforcing the sense of partnership. These shared celebrations create lasting memories and contribute to a positive and supportive relationship dynamic

---

EMBARKING ON A JOURNEY of shared life visions is a crucial aspect of building lasting compatibility in a relationship. It transcends the individual and requires a collaborative effort to weave aspirations into a shared narrative. Let's navigate this path, emphasizing transparency, compromise, and practicality for a harmonious journey together.

Understanding Individual Life Visions:

Before aligning life visions, fostering a deep understanding of individual aspirations is paramount. Open and transparent communication about personal values, career ambitions, family desires, and lifestyle preferences sets the stage for alignment. Recognizing and respecting each other's unique visions becomes the foundation for a unified life narrative.

Initiate Transparent Conversations:

- Encourage open discussions about long-term goals and aspirations.
- Cultivate an environment that promotes genuine sharing and understanding.

Identifying Commonalities:

- Seek areas where individual visions naturally align.
- Emphasize shared values and aspirations as a basis for alignment.

Respecting Differences and Compromising

Acknowledging and respecting differences is integral to the process of aligning life visions. Successful alignment often involves compromise, a delicate negotiation process where both partners feel heard and understood. This respectful approach fosters a balanced and sustainable shared life vision.

Openly Discuss Differences:

- Acknowledge and openly discuss any differing life visions.
- Cultivate an atmosphere where differences are viewed as opportunities for growth.

Seeking Compromise:

- Encourage a collaborative approach to finding common ground.
- Emphasize the importance of compromise in building a shared life vision.

Creating Milestones and Timelines

Solidifying alignment requires translating shared visions into actionable steps. Establishing concrete milestones and timelines provides direction and purpose, transforming the shared vision into a practical roadmap for both partners.

Define Realistic Milestones:

- Establish concrete milestones that contribute to the shared narrative.
- Ensure these milestones are realistic, achievable, and reflect shared values.

Setting Practical Timelines:

- Define timelines for achieving shared milestones collaboratively.
- Emphasize the importance of a practical and flexible approach to timelines.

By understanding individual aspirations transparently, embracing differences through respectful compromise, and translating shared visions into practical milestones, couples can fortify their compatibility. This strategic and practical approach not only strengthens the relationship but also lays a robust foundation for a fulfilling and enduring partnership.

Expressing Affection Authentically

THE AUTHENTICITY OF expressing affection is the linchpin for fostering genuine and deep connections. It's not merely about the actions themselves but about the sincerity that permeates those expressions. Let's explore the nuances of communicating affection in ways that feel truly genuine.

Crafting Authentic Expressions:

Authenticity in expressing affection begins with a genuine connection to your emotions. Instead of relying on generic gestures, consider what truly resonates with you and your partner. Authentic expressions stem from a place of sincerity and emotional connection, making them more meaningful and impactful.

Avoiding Generic Clichés:

While there's a place for classic expressions of affection, authenticity thrives in uniqueness. Avoid falling into the trap of clichés or generic gestures that might lack personal resonance. Tailor your expressions to your partner's preferences and the unique dynamics of your relationship, ensuring they genuinely reflect your feelings.

Open Communication About Preferences:

Authenticity is also about aligning your expressions with your partner's preferences. Engage in open and honest communication about what forms of affection feel most genuine and meaningful to both of you. Understanding each other's love language creates a foundation for authentic gestures that resonate on a deeper level.

Spontaneity and Thoughtfulness:

Authentic expressions often emerge in spontaneous moments or thoughtful gestures. Instead of adhering to a strict script, let your affection flow naturally. Surprise your partner with gestures that showcase your thoughtfulness, proving that your expressions are not merely routine but stem from a genuine desire to make them feel loved.

Customizing Expressions to the Relationship:

Every relationship is unique, and so should be the expressions of affection within it. Consider the specific dynamics, inside jokes, and shared experiences that define your connection. Customizing your expressions to the intricacies of your relationship reinforces the authenticity of your affectionate gestures.

Reflective Gestures of Understanding:

Authentic affection involves a deep understanding of your partner's emotional landscape. Reflect on their needs, desires, and the moments that bring them joy. Crafting gestures that mirror this understanding not only showcases your authenticity but also strengthens the emotional connection between you and your partner.

Expressing affection authentically is an ongoing process that requires self-awareness, open communication, and a genuine desire to connect. By crafting expressions that stem from a sincere place, avoiding generic clichés, and customizing gestures to the unique nature of your relationship, you pave the way for a bond that is not just affectionate but deeply authentic.

IT'S OFTEN THE SMALL gestures that wield the greatest power in building intimacy. These seemingly modest actions carry a profound impact, creating a tapestry of connection that goes beyond grand gestures. Let's unravel the significance of incorporating small, meaningful acts into the fabric of your relationship.

Creating Daily Connection:

Small gestures serve as daily touchpoints that create a consistent connection between partners. Whether it's a warm smile, a gentle touch, or a thoughtful note, these actions contribute to the emotional closeness that defines intimacy. By incorporating them into your daily routine, you infuse your relationship with a sense of care and attention.

Fostering Emotional Safety:

The subtlety of small gestures creates a safe space for emotional vulnerability. When partners consistently engage in these acts, it builds a foundation of trust and comfort. Knowing that your partner pays attention to the details and responds with kindness fosters an environment where both individuals feel emotionally secure and understood.

Expressing Thoughtfulness:

Small gestures are a canvas for expressing thoughtfulness. It's the little things, like remembering a favorite snack or surprising your partner with a cup of coffee, that convey a deeper level of consideration. These acts communicate that you're attuned to your partner's preferences and actively invest in making their day a bit brighter.

Cultivating Appreciation:

In the busyness of life, it's easy to overlook the significance of small gestures. Yet, these acts play a crucial role in cultivating appreciation. Whether it's a word of affirmation, a small gift, or a gesture of assistance, they communicate that you value and appreciate your partner. This mutual acknowledgment strengthens the emotional bond between you.

Building Rituals of Connection:

Small gestures can evolve into cherished rituals that define your relationship. Whether it's a goodnight kiss, a shared morning routine, or a specific way of saying "I love you," these rituals contribute to the unique identity of your connection. They serve as anchors, creating a sense of stability and predictability within the relationship.

Integrating Affection into Daily Life:

Intimacy thrives when affection becomes an integral part of daily life. Small gestures seamlessly weave affection into the fabric of your relationship. From holding hands during a walk to leaving a sweet note on the mirror, these acts transcend routine and infuse your daily interactions with a touch of love and tenderness.

Deepening Emotional Connection:

The cumulative effect of small gestures is a deepening emotional connection. It's the consistent investment in these acts that forges a bond rooted in intimacy. By expressing love and care through everyday gestures, partners contribute to an emotional richness that sustains and nurtures the relationship over time.

The power of small gestures lies in their ability to create a mosaic of intimacy. These acts, when woven together, form a tapestry that reflects care, thoughtfulness, and a genuine desire to connect. By recognizing and valuing the significance of these small gestures, couples pave the way for a relationship that is not only intimate but also resilient and enduring.

UNDERSTANDING AND SPEAKING each other's love language is a transformative key to deep connection and fulfillment. Let's delve into the significance of discovering one's unique love language and how this awareness becomes a guiding compass for expressing and receiving love.

Defining Love Languages:

Love languages are the unique ways individuals prefer to give and receive love. Recognized by Gary Chapman, they encompass words of affirmation, acts of service, receiving gifts, quality time, and physical touch. Identifying your love language, as well as your partner's, opens a doorway to a more intentional and harmonious relationship.

Self-Reflection and Awareness:

Discovering your unique love language begins with self-reflection and a keen awareness of what truly resonates with you emotionally. Pay attention to the gestures or expressions that make you feel loved and valued. Understanding your own preferences lays the foundation for effective communication with your partner.

Open Communication with Your Partner:

The journey to finding one's love language is a collaborative effort. Engage in open and honest communication with your partner about your emotional needs and preferences. Share insights into the specific actions or expressions that make you feel cherished. Similarly, encourage your partner to express their preferences.

Recognizing Acts of Love:

Often, love languages manifest through actions more than words. Pay attention to the gestures your partner employs to express love. It could be a supportive act, spending quality time together, or offering words of affirmation. Observing these actions provides valuable clues to deciphering your partner's love language.

Experimenting with Expressions:

The process of finding one's love language involves experimentation and receptivity. Be open to trying different ways of expressing love and observe how they resonate with you. Similarly, encourage your partner to explore various forms of expression. This mutual exploration strengthens the understanding of each other's unique love languages.

Flexibility and Adaptation:

As individuals evolve, so can their love languages. It's crucial to be flexible and adaptive in recognizing that preferences may change over time. Stay attuned to shifts in what makes you feel loved and inquire about any changes in your partner's preferences. This adaptability contributes to the ongoing health of the relationship.

Celebrating Diversity in Love Languages:

Every individual has a unique combination of love languages. Embrace and celebrate the diversity in how you and your partner express and receive love. Recognize the beauty in having different love languages and appreciate the richness it brings to your relationship.

Integrating Love Languages into Daily Life:

The true impact of discovering love languages is witnessed when they are seamlessly integrated into daily interactions. Incorporate your partner's love language into routine expressions of affection. Whether it's a heartfelt compliment, a small act of service, or quality time spent together, these daily gestures solidify the connection.

Finding one's unique love language is a journey of self-discovery and shared exploration within a relationship. It requires self-awareness, open communication, flexibility, and a genuine appreciation for the diverse ways individuals experience and express love. By understanding and honoring each other's love languages, couples lay the groundwork for a relationship that is deeply connected, mutually fulfilling, and resilient over time.

Navigating Vulnerability Together

EMBRACING VULNERABILITY becomes a powerful catalyst for deepening intimacy and fortifying connections. Let's explore the significance of encouraging mutual vulnerability and how it forms the bedrock of navigating challenges together.

Creating a Safe Space:

Encouraging mutual vulnerability begins with creating a safe and non-judgmental space within the relationship. Cultivate an environment where both partners feel secure in sharing their innermost thoughts, fears, and emotions without fear of criticism or rejection. This safe space lays the foundation for authentic and open communication.

Initiating Open Conversations:

Initiate open and honest conversations about feelings, concerns, and aspirations. Encourage your partner to express their thoughts and emotions without reservation. Actively listen with empathy, seeking to understand their perspective. By fostering an atmosphere of openness, you pave the way for mutual vulnerability to thrive.

Sharing Personal Experiences:

Lead by example in sharing your own vulnerabilities and personal experiences. When you reveal aspects of yourself that may be perceived as weaknesses, it fosters a sense of trust and reciprocity. Sharing your own vulnerabilities communicates that it's safe for your partner to do the same, creating a bond built on authenticity.

Avoiding Judgment and Criticism:

In the pursuit of mutual vulnerability, it's crucial to avoid judgment or criticism. Acknowledge and appreciate the courage it takes for your partner to be vulnerable. Respond with empathy and understanding, creating a supportive atmosphere that encourages further openness. This lack of judgment establishes a framework for enduring intimacy.

Expressing Empathy and Support:

Encouraging mutual vulnerability involves expressing empathy and providing support when your partner shares their vulnerabilities. Offer reassurance, understanding, and affirmation. Knowing that they can rely on your support strengthens the emotional connection, fostering an environment where both partners feel valued and accepted.

Building Trust Gradually:

Mutual vulnerability is intricately linked to trust. Building trust gradually involves consistently demonstrating that vulnerabilities will be met with compassion and care. As trust deepens, so does the willingness to be vulnerable. It's a reciprocal process where each partner contributes to the emotional safety within the relationship.

Setting Healthy Boundaries:

While encouraging vulnerability, it's essential to establish and respect healthy boundaries. Understand the comfort levels of both partners and refrain from pressuring each other to disclose more than they are comfortable sharing. Respecting boundaries contributes to a sense of autonomy within vulnerability.

Promoting Growth and Connection:

The beauty of mutual vulnerability lies in its ability to promote growth and strengthen the connection between partners. When both individuals feel safe to expose their true selves, it creates a dynamic where personal and relational development can flourish. Shared vulnerability becomes a transformative force that propels the relationship forward.

Encouraging mutual vulnerability is a dynamic process that involves communication, empathy, and the cultivation of a safe space. By initiating open conversations, sharing personal experiences, avoiding judgment, expressing empathy, and gradually building trust, couples pave the way for an intimate connection that thrives on authenticity and shared growth. Mutual vulnerability becomes not only a pathway through challenges but a cornerstone for a relationship that stands resilient over time.

CHALLENGES ARE AN UNAVOIDABLE part of the journey. However, the resilience of a partnership lies in the strategic approach taken to navigate these challenges collaboratively. Let's explore actionable strategies aligned with effective online writing principles for facing and overcoming obstacles together.

1. **Establishing Open Communication:**

- **Strategic Communication:** Cultivate a culture of transparent and strategic communication within the relationship.

Foster an environment where constructive dialogue thrives, laying the groundwork for a mutual understanding of perspectives.

1. **Active Listening and Empathy:**

- **Intentional Listening:** Embrace the art of intentional listening, seeking to understand your partner's feelings and concerns.

Approach challenging situations with empathy, recognizing diverse experiences, and fostering a united front.

1. **Collaborative Problem-Solving:**

- **Joint Puzzle-Solving:** Treat challenges as joint puzzles, engaging in collaborative problem-solving.

Convey challenges as opportunities for joint growth and problem-solving, emphasizing unity in overcoming obstacles.

1. **Understanding Individual Coping Mechanisms:**

- **Respecting Differences:** Understand and respect diverse coping mechanisms, acknowledging individuality.

Recognize and appreciate differences in coping mechanisms, fostering harmony during challenging times.

1. **Building Resilience Through Shared Goals:**

- **Collective Vision:** Establish shared goals as beacons of resilience during challenges.

Instill a sense of purpose through shared goals, emphasizing the larger vision of the relationship.

1. **Seeking Professional Support When Needed:**

- **External Expertise:** Recognize when external expertise is beneficial, seeking professional support when necessary.

Advocate for seeking guidance from professionals, providing a comprehensive approach to navigating complex challenges.

1. **Taking Breaks to Regain Perspective:**

- **Mindful Breaks:** Acknowledge the importance of mindful breaks to regain perspective during challenging moments.

Encourage breaks as a strategy to maintain a clear mindset and prevent escalation during online discussions.

1. **Celebrating Small Victories:**

- **Incremental Achievements:** Acknowledge and celebrate small victories as incremental achievements.

Reinforce a positive atmosphere by highlighting and celebrating progress, no matter how small.

1. **Forging a Uniting Narrative:**

- **Strengthening Bonds:** Frame challenges as opportunities for growth, emphasizing the strength of the partnership.

Cultivate a uniting narrative that views challenges as moments to strengthen the bond between partners.

1. **Nurturing Self-Care and Mutual Support:**

- **Balanced Approach:** Encourage a balanced approach to self-care and mutual support during challenging times.

Promote self-care practices and mutual support online, recognizing the importance of individual well-being.

Effective strategies for navigating challenges online involve strategic communication, intentional listening, collaborative problem-solving, and fostering resilience through shared goals. By aligning with the principles of online writing, these strategies contribute to building a resilient foundation that not only withstands challenges but strengthens the fabric of the relationship over time.

The Impact of Shared Vulnerability on Intimacy

EMBRACING SHARED VULNERABILITY emerges as a transformative force, profoundly influencing the depth of intimacy between partners. Let's explore this impactful journey through essential questions and answers, complemented by strategic insights.

1. How does shared vulnerability strengthen emotional bonds?

Shared Vulnerability as a Bonding Agent:

- Opening up about vulnerabilities is a shared journey, creating a profound sense of connection. Partners who share their innermost thoughts and fears build emotional bonds that go beyond surface-level interactions.

Fostering Deeper Emotional Bonds:

- This act of sharing vulnerabilities fosters a unique understanding, creating a deeper emotional connection. The vulnerability exchanged becomes a testament to the authenticity that defines the relationship.

2. Why is trust an integral component of shared vulnerability?

Foundation of Trust:

- Trust is a cornerstone as partners allow themselves to be vulnerable, knowing their authenticity is accepted. Shared vulnerability becomes the bedrock, contributing to a relationship where partners feel secure and understood.

Establishing a Safe Space:

- The shared vulnerabilities establish a safe space, free from judgment. Trust flourishes as this space becomes a haven for open communication and mutual understanding.

3. How does shared vulnerability create a culture of acceptance?

Embracing Imperfections:

- Cultivating a culture where imperfections are embraced is a key outcome of shared vulnerability. Partners learn to appreciate and love each other authentically.

Nurturing Authentic Connections:

- Acceptance grows as partners witness and share vulnerabilities, creating an authentic connection that transcends societal expectations.

4. In what ways does shared vulnerability deepen emotional intimacy?

Authenticity Breeds Intimacy:

- The authenticity in shared vulnerability is a catalyst for deepening emotional intimacy. Partners feel a unique closeness when they can be their true selves without fear of judgment.

Connecting Through Shared Experiences:

- Shared vulnerabilities create experiences that form the fabric of emotional intimacy. Partners connect on a profound level, knowing they have shared their innermost selves.

5. How does shared vulnerability contribute to effective communication?

Open Communication:

- Shared vulnerability enhances communication by creating a space where partners can openly express thoughts and feelings. Partners feel more comfortable discussing challenging topics, leading to a deeper understanding.

Fostering a Culture of Honesty:

- The act of being vulnerable fosters a culture of honesty and transparency. Effective communication becomes a natural outcome as partners navigate shared vulnerabilities.

The impact of shared vulnerability on intimacy is a dynamic and transformative journey that strengthens emotional bonds, builds trust, fosters a culture of acceptance, deepens emotional intimacy, and enhances communication. Through the lens of essential questions and strategic insights, we unravel the profound significance of shared vulnerability in creating a rich and fulfilling intimacy within relationships.

AS WE CONCLUDE OUR exploration into the art of creating intimate connections, it's essential to distill the key takeaways that will serve as guiding principles for building relationships that withstand the test of time.

1. Prioritize Emotional Intimacy:

- **Differentiate Between Physical and Emotional Intimacy:** Recognize that true connection goes beyond the physical realm, emphasizing the importance of emotional intimacy.

- **Foster Deeper Connections:** Understand how emotional intimacy fosters profound connections that form the foundation of lasting relationships.

- **Nurture Emotional Intimacy in Dating:** Actively nurture emotional intimacy during the dating phase, laying the groundwork for a meaningful connection.

2. Cultivate Trust Gradually:

- **Recognize the Role of Trust:** Acknowledge that trust is the cornerstone of intimate connections, creating a sense of security and openness.

- **Strategically Build Trust Over Time:** Implement effective strategies for gradually building trust, understanding that trust is a dynamic and evolving aspect of relationships.

- **Address Trust Issues:** Be proactive in recognizing and addressing trust issues, fostering a relationship environment grounded in trust and reliability.

3. **Embrace Shared Values and Goals:**

- **Identify and Discuss Core Values:** Engage in open conversations to identify and discuss core values, ensuring alignment for a strong and enduring connection.

- **Strengthen Connections Through Shared Goals:** Understand the power of shared goals in fortifying connections, creating a sense of purpose and unity.

- **Align Life Visions:** Ensure lasting compatibility by aligning life visions, fostering a future that both partners envision together.

4. **Express Affection Authentically:**

- **Communicate Genuine Affection:** Learn the art of communicating affection in ways that feel genuine and meaningful.

- **Harness the Power of Small Gestures:** Recognize the impact of small gestures in building intimacy, appreciating the significance of these seemingly minor actions.

- **Discover Unique Love Languages:** Understand and embrace each other's unique love language, enhancing the authenticity of your expressions of love.

5. Navigate Vulnerability Together:

- **Encourage Mutual Vulnerability:** Foster an environment that encourages mutual vulnerability, recognizing it as a powerful catalyst for deepening connection.

- **Strategize for Navigating Challenges:** Implement effective strategies for navigating challenges together, understanding that facing adversity strengthens the fabric of the relationship.

- **Embrace the Impact of Shared Vulnerability:** Reflect on how shared vulnerability contributes to the overall intimacy of the relationship, creating a dynamic where authenticity thrives.

In essence, creating intimate connections is a deliberate and nuanced journey. By prioritizing emotional intimacy, cultivating trust, embracing shared values, expressing affection authentically, and navigating vulnerability together, you lay the groundwork for a relationship that stands resilient against the trials of time. These key takeaways serve as a roadmap for building connections that are not only deep and meaningful but also enduring and fulfilling. As you embark on your journey of love and connection, remember these principles, and may your relationships flourish and endure.

Balancing Alone Time Or Socializing

Chapter 7

"Me-time or We-time? Have you ever wondered if the key to a thriving relationship lies in mastering the art of solitude and socializing? Let's explore the answer together."

The Value of Alone Time

RECOGNIZING AND RESPECTING personal space emerges as a fundamental pillar for building a strong foundation. The journey begins with a profound acknowledgment that each individual brings a unique essence to the relationship, one that flourishes in the nurturing embrace of personal space.

Understanding the Essence of Personal Space:

Personal space is not merely physical distance; it encompasses the emotional and psychological breathing room that individuals require to thrive independently. It's about recognizing that both partners have distinct identities, aspirations, and moments of solitude that contribute to their well-being.

The Role of Personal Space in Relationship Dynamics:

Acknowledging the importance of personal space is akin to honoring the individual narratives within the relationship. It paves the way for a balanced partnership, where each person's autonomy is respected, fostering a sense of self within the shared journey.

Building Mutual Respect:

Recognizing personal space lays the groundwork for mutual respect. It's an understanding that in valuing your partner's need for solitude, you contribute to their growth and well-being. This shared respect becomes a cornerstone for a healthy and fulfilling connection.

Preventing Emotional Burnout:

In the hustle and bustle of daily life, recognizing personal space becomes a shield against emotional burnout. Allowing moments for individual reflection and rejuvenation becomes an investment in the long-term emotional health of the relationship.

Creating an Environment of Trust:

The acknowledgment of personal space cultivates an environment of trust. When partners feel secure in their individuality, the trust within the relationship deepens, fostering an atmosphere of openness and vulnerability.

Balancing Togetherness and Independence:

Recognizing personal space doesn't diminish the value of togetherness. Instead, it enhances it by striking a delicate balance between shared moments and individual pursuits. This equilibrium is the key to a relationship that thrives on both unity and diversity.

Recognizing the importance of personal space is not a step back from intimacy but a significant leap forward in building a resilient and flourishing connection. It's an affirmation that in honoring individuality, we fortify the collective strength of the relationship. As we navigate the intricacies of recognizing personal space, let's embrace the wisdom that lies in understanding, respecting, and celebrating the unique essence each partner brings to the shared journey.

IN THE HUSTLE AND BUSTLE of modern life, carving out space for healthy alone time within a relationship is not only beneficial but essential for individual well-being and the overall health of the partnership. Let's delve into practical strategies that foster a harmonious blend of togetherness and solitude.

1. Scheduled 'Me-Time' Rituals:

- Establish dedicated time slots for personal pursuits. Whether it's pursuing hobbies, reading, or simply quiet contemplation, having a regularly scheduled 'me-time' creates a structured and predictable space for individual rejuvenation.

2. Communication and Coordination:

- Open and transparent communication is key. Discuss with your partner the need for alone time and coordinate schedules to ensure that both individuals have ample opportunities for solitary activities without encroaching on each other's space.

3. Designated Personal Spaces:

- Create physical spaces within your shared environment that serve as personal retreats. It could be a cozy reading nook, a home office, or a corner for artistic expression. Having designated areas for alone time reinforces the idea of shared spaces coexisting with individual sanctuaries.

4. Solo Adventures and Outings:

- Encourage each other to embark on solo adventures or outings. Whether it's exploring a new hobby, attending a workshop, or simply taking a solo day trip, these experiences contribute to personal growth and allow for independent exploration.

5.Respect Each Other's Rhythms:

- Understand and respect your partner's natural rhythms and energy levels. Some individuals recharge through social interactions, while others thrive in moments of quiet solitude. By acknowledging these differences, you can synchronize your activities to complement each other's needs.

6. Digital Detox Together:

- Consider implementing occasional digital detox sessions where both partners disconnect from technology. This not only allows for a break from external stimuli but also creates an environment conducive to meaningful connection during shared activities.

7.Encourage Pursuit of Passions:

- Support and encourage your partner's pursuit of individual passions and interests. Whether it's a creative endeavor, a fitness goal, or personal development, fostering each other's growth contributes to a richer and more fulfilling relationship.

8.Reflection and Check-Ins:

- Regularly reflect on your alone time routines and assess their impact on your well-being and the relationship. Conduct check-ins with your partner to ensure that the strategies in place are meeting both your individual needs and the collective goals of the relationship.

Incorporating healthy alone time in relationships is not about creating distance but about fostering an environment where both partners can thrive individually, contributing to a stronger and more resilient connection when together. By implementing these strategies, you'll embark on a journey that embraces the beauty of solitude within the context of a flourishing relationship.

EFFECTIVE COMMUNICATION of personal boundaries is the cornerstone of a healthy and thriving relationship. It not only ensures that each partner feels respected and understood but also sets the stage for a harmonious connection. Let's explore actionable strategies for articulating and respecting personal boundaries within the context of a relationship.

1. **Self-Reflection and Awareness:**

• Begin by engaging in self-reflection to identify your own boundaries. Understand your needs, preferences, and limits. This self-awareness lays the foundation for clear and intentional communication with your partner.

1. **Choose an Appropriate Setting:**

• When initiating a conversation about personal boundaries, choose a setting that is conducive to open communication. Opt for a quiet and private space where both partners can focus on the discussion without distractions.

1. **Use "I" Statements:**

• Frame your boundaries using "I" statements to express your feelings and needs without sounding accusatory. For example, "I feel more energized when I have some quiet time in the evenings."

1. **Be Specific and Concrete:**

• Clearly articulate your boundaries with specificity. Vague statements may lead to misunderstandings. Instead of saying, "I need more space," specify what that space looks like in practical terms.

1. **Express Boundaries Positively:**

• Frame your boundaries in a positive light. Instead of saying what you don't want, express what you do want. For instance, "I appreciate when we have dedicated time for personal activities."

1. **Use Clear Examples:**

• Illustrate your boundaries with concrete examples. This helps your partner understand the practical application of the boundaries you're expressing. Real-life scenarios make the conversation more relatable.

1. **Discuss and Negotiate:**

• Encourage an open dialogue where both partners can discuss their boundaries. Be open to negotiation and compromise, ensuring that the final agreement is mutually beneficial and respects the needs of both individuals.

1. **Establish Non-Negotiables:**

• Identify certain boundaries that are non-negotiable for you. Clearly communicate these limits to your partner, emphasizing their importance to your well-being and the health of the relationship.

1. **Check-In Periodically:**

• Personal boundaries may evolve over time. Schedule periodic check-ins with your partner to reassess and discuss any adjustments or changes to your boundaries. This ongoing communication ensures that both individuals feel heard and understood.

1. **Be a Respectful Listener:**

• Actively listen to your partner's boundaries with the same level of respect and consideration you expect for your own. Validate their feelings and demonstrate a willingness to understand and accommodate their needs.

Remember, effective communication of personal boundaries is a dynamic process that requires ongoing attention and collaboration. By approaching this aspect of your relationship with openness, clarity, and empathy, you lay the groundwork for a partnership where both individuals can thrive and feel valued.

Socializing with Comfort

EVER FOUND YOURSELF in a sea of social interactions, grappling with discomfort and uncertainty? The journey to socializing with ease is not a daunting quest but a skill that can be honed. Let's embark on the voyage of mastering social comfort together.

Social anxiety in group settings can be challenging, but with practical strategies and a mindful approach, it's possible to navigate social interactions with increased confidence. Here are effective tips for managing social anxiety and fostering a sense of comfort in group settings:

1. **Prepare and Set Realistic Expectations:**

Anticipate social situations by preparing mentally. Set realistic expectations for yourself, acknowledging that not every interaction needs to be flawless. Embrace imperfections as part of the human experience.

1. **Focus on the Present Moment:**

Ground yourself in the present moment. Instead of worrying about future interactions or past perceived mistakes, channel your attention to what is happening in the here and now. Mindfulness techniques, such as deep breathing, can be invaluable in staying present.

1. **Start with Small, Manageable Groups:**

Gradually expose yourself to social situations by starting with smaller groups. This allows you to practice socializing in a more controlled environment, gradually building your comfort level.

1. **Establish a Socialization Routine:**

Create a routine for socialization. Having a consistent pattern can provide a sense of familiarity and reduce anxiety. For example, always arriving early to events or engaging in brief, casual conversations can become part of your routine.

1. **Challenge Negative Thoughts:**

Challenge negative thoughts that contribute to social anxiety. Identify and reframe irrational beliefs, replacing them with more balanced and positive perspectives. Cognitive-behavioral techniques can be useful in restructuring thought patterns.

1. **Set Realistic Social Goals:**

Establish realistic social goals for yourself. Instead of aiming for perfection, focus on achievable objectives such as initiating a conversation with one new person or actively participating in a group discussion.

1. **Use Visualization Techniques:**

Visualize successful social interactions. Imagine yourself navigating group settings with ease and confidence. Visualization can help rewire your brain to associate social situations with positive outcomes.

1. **Seek Support from a Trusted Friend:**

Attend social events with a trusted friend who understands your challenges. Having a supportive companion can provide a safety net and make socializing less daunting.

1. **Take Breaks When Needed:**

Allow yourself breaks during social events. Stepping away briefly to collect your thoughts can prevent feelings of overwhelm and contribute to a more positive overall experience.

1. **Celebrate Small Victories:**

   Acknowledge and celebrate small victories. Each successful social interaction, no matter how minor, is a step toward building confidence. Recognize and appreciate your progress.

By incorporating these tips into your approach to socializing, you can gradually manage social anxiety and cultivate a greater sense of ease in group settings. Remember, the journey to social comfort is unique to each individual, and progress is achieved one step at a time.

Misconceptions About Cultivating Ease During Social Events

MISCONCEPTION: BEING Socially Comfortable Means Being Extroverted:

Social comfort is not synonymous with extroversion. Introverts can cultivate ease by finding environments that align with their preferences and using strategies that honor their need for solitude. Comfort in social events is about authenticity, not conforming to extroverted norms.

Misconception: If You're Anxious, You're Doing Something Wrong:

Anxiety in social situations is common and doesn't imply failure. It's a natural response to unfamiliar or challenging scenarios. Acknowledging and working through anxiety, rather than viewing it as a flaw, is a step toward cultivating genuine ease during social events.

Misconception: You Have to Be the Center of Attention to Enjoy Socializing:

Enjoying social events doesn't require being the life of the party. Meaningful connections can happen in smaller, more intimate settings. Cultivating ease involves finding the balance that suits you, whether it's engaging in deep conversations with a few people or enjoying the energy of a larger group from a comfortable distance.

Misconception: Social Comfort Is an All-or-Nothing Achievement:

Social comfort is a journey, not a destination. It's unrealistic to expect immediate, complete ease in all social situations. Progress often comes in small steps. Recognizing and celebrating incremental successes contributes to an overall sense of ease over time.

Misconception: Socializing Should Always Be Effortless:

Effort is a natural part of socializing, especially for those managing anxiety. Putting in effort to apply strategies, set realistic goals, and practice self-compassion doesn't mean you're doing it wrong. It signifies a commitment to personal growth and building social ease gradually.

Misconception: Being Alone Equals Loneliness:

Enjoying alone time doesn't equate to loneliness. It's an essential aspect of self-care and personal recharge. Cultivating ease during social events involves appreciating both alone time and social interactions, finding a harmonious balance that aligns with your preferences.

Misconception: Others Are Judging You Harshly:

People are generally more focused on themselves than on scrutinizing others. The fear of judgment is often exaggerated. Remember that everyone has their insecurities and is navigating their own social dynamics. Most individuals are more empathetic and understanding than we might assume.

Misconception: Socializing Requires Constant High Energy:

Sustainable socializing involves recognizing and respecting your energy levels. It's okay to take breaks, recharge, and participate at a pace that feels comfortable. Social comfort is about finding a rhythm that aligns with your natural energy flow.

Misconception: Success in Socializing Means Pleasing Everyone:

You don't need to please everyone to succeed in social situations. Focus on genuine connections and being true to yourself rather than trying to meet everyone's expectations. Authenticity often leads to more meaningful and lasting connections.

Misconception: Cultivating Social Comfort Is a Solo Journey:

Building social ease doesn't mean navigating it alone. Seek support from friends, share experiences, and be open about your journey. Connecting with others who understand can provide valuable insights, encouragement, and a sense of community.

By dispelling these misconceptions, you pave the way for a more realistic and compassionate approach to cultivating ease during social events. Embracing the uniqueness of your journey and understanding that social comfort is a nuanced and evolving process contributes to a healthier and more enjoyable social experience.

Communicating Socializing Preferences with Clarity and Respect

EFFECTIVELY COMMUNICATING your socializing preferences is crucial for fostering understanding and creating an environment that aligns with your needs. Here's a guide on how to express your preferences with clarity and respect:

1. Self-Reflection:

- Before communicating your preferences, take time for self-reflection. Understand the types of social interactions you enjoy, the environments that make you comfortable, and any boundaries you'd like to establish. This self-awareness lays the foundation for clear communication.

2. Choose an Appropriate Time:

- Select an appropriate time to discuss socializing preferences. Opt for a calm moment when both you and your partner or social group can engage in a thoughtful conversation without distractions. Avoid bringing up the topic in the midst of a social event or when emotions are heightened.

3. Use "I" Statements:

- Frame your preferences using "I" statements to express your feelings and needs without sounding accusatory. For example, say, "I feel more at ease in smaller gatherings" instead of "You always choose large events, and I hate them."

4. Be Specific and Concrete:

- Clearly articulate your preferences with specificity. Instead of vague statements, provide concrete examples. For instance, say, "I prefer casual one-on-one conversations or small group outings" to convey a specific preference that others can understand and respect.

5. Express Positivity:

- Frame your preferences in a positive light. Emphasize the types of social interactions you enjoy rather than focusing solely on what you want to avoid. Positivity creates an open and receptive atmosphere for discussion.

6. Share Your Reasons:

- Offer insights into the reasons behind your preferences. This could involve explaining how certain social settings energize you or expressing a desire for more meaningful connections. Providing context helps others understand your perspective.

7. Be Open to Compromise:

- Acknowledge that social preferences may differ among individuals. Be open to finding a middle ground or compromise that respects everyone's comfort. This collaborative approach fosters understanding and strengthens relationships.

8. Use Non-Verbal Cues:

- Sometimes, non-verbal cues can complement verbal communication. If you're in a social setting and feeling overwhelmed, use subtle gestures or cues to communicate your comfort level to those around you. This could include stepping aside for a moment or making eye contact with a trusted friend.

9. Offer Alternatives:

- Suggest alternative social activities or settings that align with your preferences. Proposing alternatives shows your willingness to engage while offering options that make you feel more at ease.

10. Reinforce Appreciation:

- Express gratitude for the understanding and support of those you're communicating with. Reinforce that your goal is to enhance the quality of your interactions, and you appreciate their willingness to consider your preferences..

Remember, effective communication is a two-way street. Encourage open dialogue, actively listen to others' preferences, and collaborate to create social environments that are enjoyable for everyone involved. By approaching these conversations with respect and consideration, you contribute to a more harmonious and understanding social landscape.

Creating Quality Time Together

"HAVE YOU EVER ENVISIONED your shared moments as chapters in a beautiful story? Explore the art of crafting quality time together, turning every page into a narrative of love, laughter, and enduring connection."

Finding the equilibrium between socializing and cherishing intimate moments is a delicate art. It involves understanding the dynamics of group interactions and the profound connection that blossoms in one-on-one settings. So, how do you strike the right balance to ensure your relationships thrive? Let's dive into the essence of balancing socializing with meaningful one-on-one time.

Why It Matters:

Each thread contributes to the overall picture. Meaningful one-on-one time serves as the intricate weave that adds depth and intimacy. It provides a space for genuine conversations, shared laughter, and the kind of connection that strengthens the foundation of your relationship.

Nurturing Bonds in Social Settings:

Socializing is the heartbeat of relationships, bringing vibrancy and shared experiences. Whether it's group outings, gatherings, or events, these moments create a shared history. However, the key lies in complementing these social interactions with pockets of one-on-one time. This intentional balance allows you to delve deeper into individual connections amid the social buzz.

Strategies for Effective Balance:

1. **Scheduled Quality Time:** Dedicate specific moments for one-on-one interactions in your schedule. This could be a weekly dinner, a weekend getaway, or even a quiet evening at home. Scheduling reinforces the importance of individual connection.

1. **Open Communication:** Discuss your preferences and the need for one-on-one time openly with your partner or loved ones. Transparency creates understanding, fostering an environment where both socializing and intimate moments are valued.

1. **Mixing Social and Intimate Settings:** Blend social events with opportunities for one-on-one connections. For example, during a group gathering, find moments to share a private conversation or take a stroll together. This way, you seamlessly integrate both dynamics.

Benefits of a Balanced Approach:

1. **Deeper Emotional Connection:** Meaningful one-on-one time allows for deeper emotional sharing and vulnerability, strengthening your emotional bond.

1. **Enhanced Communication:** Balancing socializing and intimate moments improves communication skills, ensuring that both partners feel heard and understood.

1. **Individual Growth:** One-on-one time provides space for individual growth within the relationship, fostering a sense of independence and self-discovery.

Finding the right equilibrium between socializing and meaningful one-on-one time is an ongoing journey. It's about recognizing the unique value each dynamic brings and intentionally weaving both into the fabric of your relationships. By doing so, you create a rich and harmonious connection where shared joy flourishes both in the company of many and the embrace of one.

THE TIME YOU INVEST holds the power to shape the satisfaction and fulfillment you experience. Quality time is not merely a clock ticking; it's the heartbeat of connection, weaving a narrative that contributes significantly to the satisfaction within a relationship. Let's delve into the profound impact that intentional quality time can have on relationship satisfaction.

Creating a Strong Foundation:

Quality time serves as the cornerstone upon which the foundation of a relationship is laid. It involves being fully present, engaged, and invested in each other's company. Whether it's through shared activities, meaningful conversations, or quiet moments, this dedicated time builds the framework for a satisfying and resilient bond.

Fostering Emotional Connection:

The essence of quality time lies in the depth of emotional connection it cultivates. When partners or loved ones consistently spend meaningful moments together, they create a shared emotional landscape. This emotional intimacy is a key driver of relationship satisfaction, fostering a sense of belonging, understanding, and support.

Quality Over Quantity:

It's not about the sheer quantity of time spent but the quality of those moments. A few hours of genuine connection can surpass days of mere proximity. The impact of quality time is magnified when both individuals feel seen, heard, and valued during these shared experiences.

Building Positive Memories:

The moments you share contribute to a treasury of shared memories. Positive experiences, laughter, and overcoming challenges together create a reservoir of joy that can be revisited during tougher times. These shared memories serve as anchors, reminding partners of the satisfaction derived from their time together.

Mitigating Relationship Stress:

Quality time acts as a counterbalance to the stresses and challenges relationships inevitably face. When partners intentionally carve out time for each other, it becomes a haven where they can escape daily pressures, reconnect, and rejuvenate their connection. This proactive approach to stress management enhances overall relationship satisfaction.

Cultivating Mutual Growth:

Intentional quality time provides a platform for mutual growth within a relationship. Whether it's pursuing shared hobbies, exploring new experiences, or supporting individual aspirations, these moments become catalysts for personal and collective development. The satisfaction derived from witnessing and contributing to each other's growth strengthens the fabric of the relationship.

Measuring Relationship Health:

The satisfaction derived from quality time becomes a barometer for the overall health of a relationship. When both partners consistently find fulfillment in their shared moments, it indicates a relationship that is thriving and resilient.

The impact of quality time on relationship satisfaction is profound and multifaceted. It's about creating a tapestry of shared experiences, fostering emotional connection, and actively investing in the growth and well-being of the relationship. As you navigate the intricacies of time together, remember that the intentional moments you share are not just minutes on the clock—they are the building blocks of a satisfying and enduring connection.

UNDERSTANDING AND ACCOMMODATING diverse preferences is the key to creating a harmonious melody. When it comes to planning activities, catering to both introverted and extroverted tendencies requires finesse. Let's explore the art of crafting activities that resonate with both ends of the personality spectrum, ensuring shared moments of joy for everyone involved.

Embracing Diversity in Preferences:

Introversion and extroversion represent two ends of the personality spectrum, each with its unique set of preferences and energy dynamics. Recognizing and embracing these differences lay the groundwork for planning activities that cater to the diverse needs of both introverted and extroverted individuals.

Balancing Social and Solitary Moments:

The key to accommodating both preferences lies in achieving a delicate equilibrium between social and solitary activities. A well-crafted plan seamlessly integrates moments of connection and shared experiences with intervals of personal space and reflection.

Open Communication:

Before diving into activity planning, foster open communication about individual preferences. Encourage a dialogue where each person feels comfortable expressing their needs and desires. This transparency ensures that the chosen activities align with the comfort zones of both introverted and extroverted participants.

Ideas for Inclusive Activities

1. Cozy Movie Night In:

- Create a cozy movie night at home with a carefully curated film selection. This provides the introverted individuals a relaxed and intimate setting while still allowing for shared enjoyment.

2. Nature Retreats:

- Plan outings to natural settings like parks, hiking trails, or scenic spots. Nature retreats offer a blend of outdoor adventure for the extroverts and a tranquil environment for introverts to recharge.

3. Themed Game Nights:

- Organize themed game nights that incorporate a mix of board games, trivia, or interactive video games. This caters to the extroverted love for social interaction while allowing introverts to participate at their own pace.

4. Artistic Workshops:

- Engage in artistic workshops, such as painting or crafting. This provides a creative outlet for both personality types, allowing extroverts to express themselves openly and introverts to immerse themselves in solitary creation.

5. Book Club Discussions:

- Establish a book club for literary enthusiasts. Introverts can relish the quiet pleasure of reading, while extroverts can engage in lively discussions, combining individual pursuits with shared intellectual exploration.

Flexibility in Planning:

Recognize that preferences can evolve, and flexibility is key. Be open to adjusting plans based on the energy levels and comfort of participants. The success of inclusive activities lies in creating an environment where both introverts and extroverts feel seen, heard, and valued.

Celebrating Differences:

Rather than viewing introversion and extroversion as challenges, celebrate the richness that both bring to the relationship. Acknowledge and honor the strengths each personality type contributes, creating a tapestry of experiences that cater to the diverse needs within the partnership.

Planning activities that cater to both introverted and extroverted preferences is an art of balance and understanding. By creating a repertoire of inclusive and flexible activities, you forge a path where both ends of the personality spectrum can thrive, ensuring that every shared moment becomes a source of joy and connection for everyone involved.

Honest Communication About Needs

COMMUNICATION SERVES as the navigational tool in the vast sea of relationships, guiding partners toward a harmonious balance. When it comes to establishing equilibrium between personal needs for alone time and socializing, the role of communication is paramount. Let's delve into how effective communication becomes the compass, steering relationships toward a balanced and understanding course.

Setting the Foundation:

Communication is the bedrock upon which a relationship's dynamics are built. It involves expressing desires, needs, and boundaries openly and honestly. When partners engage in effective communication, they lay the groundwork for understanding each other's individual requirements for solitude and social engagement.

Expressing Personal Needs:

The process begins with each individual expressing their personal needs regarding alone time and socializing. Whether one partner thrives in moments of solitude or the other finds energy in social interactions, open communication allows for a clear and mutual understanding of these needs.

Navigating Differences:

Differences in preferences for alone time and socializing are natural in any relationship. The role of communication is to navigate these differences with empathy and understanding. It involves finding compromise, negotiating boundaries, and ensuring that both partners feel heard and respected.

Constructive Problem-Solving:

Communication becomes a tool for constructive problem-solving. When conflicts arise around personal needs, partners can engage in open discussions to find solutions that meet both their individual requirements. This collaborative approach strengthens the bond and fosters a sense of unity in navigating the ebb and flow of personal preferences.

Creating a Supportive Environment:

The environment in which communication takes place is crucial. Partners must actively contribute to creating a safe and supportive space for open conversations. This involves fostering an atmosphere where expressing needs is encouraged, and vulnerabilities are met with understanding rather than judgment.

Establishing Regular Check-Ins:

Communication is an ongoing process that requires regular check-ins. Partners can set aside dedicated times to discuss their evolving needs, ensuring that as individuals grow and change, the relationship's dynamics adapt to accommodate those shifts.

Affirming Feelings and Needs:

Part of effective communication is affirming each other's feelings and needs. This validation creates a sense of security and acceptance, fostering an environment where partners feel comfortable expressing their authentic selves.

The role of communication in establishing balance between personal needs for alone time and socializing is transformative. It acts as the compass that not only points the way but also helps partners navigate the varied landscapes of preferences within a relationship. When communication is embraced as a tool for understanding, empathy, and problem-solving, it becomes the cornerstone of a relationship where both partners feel valued and heard.

DISCUSSIONS ABOUT PERSONAL needs for alone time and socializing are vital checkpoints on the journey to understanding and harmony. These conversations provide a platform for individuals to express their unique preferences and foster an environment where both partners feel acknowledged and respected. Let's delve into the art of navigating these discussions and creating a space where personal needs can coexist harmoniously.

Initiating Open Dialogues:

The first step in discussing personal needs is to initiate open dialogues. Create an atmosphere where both partners feel comfortable expressing their desires and boundaries regarding alone time and socializing. These conversations should be framed with a spirit of curiosity and a genuine interest in understanding each other.

Expressing the Why:

As individuals share their needs, it's equally important to express the reasons behind them. Whether someone thrives in solitude for introspection or gains energy from social interactions, understanding the "why" behind these preferences adds depth to the discussion. It fosters empathy and provides context for the partner to grasp the significance of these needs.

Seeking Compromise and Solutions:

Discussing personal needs is not about finding winners or losers but about seeking compromise and solutions that meet both individuals halfway. It involves a collaborative exploration of how alone time and socializing can coexist within the relationship. This might include setting boundaries, creating dedicated time for each need, or finding shared activities that cater to both preferences.

Establishing Communication Patterns:

Consistency in communication is key. Establish patterns for discussing personal needs regularly. This could involve periodic check-ins or creating a safe space where individuals feel free to express evolving preferences as they navigate different seasons in life.

Creating a Judgment-Free Zone:

Building a judgment-free zone is crucial for honest discussions. Individuals should feel secure in expressing their needs without fear of criticism or rejection. This zone encourages vulnerability and authenticity, laying the foundation for a relationship where both partners can thrive as their genuine selves.

Discussing personal needs for alone time and socializing is a dynamic process that requires openness, empathy, and a commitment to understanding. When approached with a spirit of collaboration, these discussions become opportunities for growth and deepening the connection within a relationship. Ultimately, they pave the way for a shared journey where personal needs can coexist, creating a tapestry woven with threads of understanding, compromise, and mutual respect.

THE ENVIRONMENT IN which conversations unfold holds the power to shape the depth and authenticity of connection. When it comes to discussing personal needs, creating a supportive atmosphere for open conversations is essential. This nurturing space becomes the catalyst for understanding, empathy, and a flourishing relationship. Let's explore the art of fostering this supportive environment.

Cultivating Emotional Safety:

At the core of a supportive environment is the cultivation of emotional safety. Partners should feel secure expressing their thoughts, feelings, and needs without fear of judgment or reprisal. This emotional safety net is the foundation upon which open and honest conversations thrive.

Active Presence and Undivided Attention:

Supportive environments are marked by active presence and undivided attention. When engaging in conversations, be fully present, setting aside distractions and genuinely focusing on the words and emotions being shared. This level of attentiveness communicates respect and validates the importance of the discussion.

Approaching with Empathy:

Empathy is the bridge that connects individuals on a deeper level. Creating a supportive environment involves approaching conversations with genuine empathy. Strive to understand your partner's perspective, acknowledge their emotions, and convey a sincere interest in comprehending their experiences.

Encouraging Vulnerability:

A supportive space encourages vulnerability—a willingness to share one's authentic self without reservation. Partners should feel comfortable expressing their thoughts, even those that may make them feel exposed. This vulnerability deepens the bond and fosters a sense of intimacy.

Avoiding Judgment and Criticism:

Judgment-free zones are characterized by an absence of criticism. In a supportive environment, partners refrain from passing judgment on each other's thoughts, feelings, or needs. Instead, the focus is on understanding and exploring solutions collaboratively.

Setting the Tone with Positivity:

Positivity sets the tone for supportive environments. Even in discussions about challenges or personal needs, maintaining a positive and constructive approach fosters a sense of optimism. This positivity contributes to an atmosphere where individuals feel encouraged to express themselves authentically.

Establishing Open-Door Policies:

Creating a supportive environment involves establishing open-door policies. Partners should feel free to initiate conversations about personal needs at any time. This accessibility contributes to an ongoing dialogue, preventing issues from festering and creating an atmosphere of openness.

Using "I" Statements:

Effective communication in a supportive space often involves using "I" statements. Framing thoughts and feelings from a personal perspective reduces defensiveness and promotes a collaborative approach to problem-solving. For example, "I feel" instead of "You always."

Reaffirming Appreciation and Love:

Even in discussions about personal needs, reaffirming appreciation and love is crucial. Remind each other of the shared values, positive aspects of the relationship, and the reasons that brought you together. This affirmation builds a foundation of love and respect.

Fostering a supportive environment for open conversations is an art that requires intention and commitment. When partners actively cultivate emotional safety, approach discussions with empathy, and maintain a positive tone, they create a space where authenticity flourishes. This supportive environment becomes the canvas on which the intricacies of personal needs are explored, understood, and woven into the fabric of a strong and resilient relationship.

Building a Supportive Relationship Network

THE CONNECTIONS WOVEN beyond the primary partnership play a vital role in fostering support, growth, and shared experiences. Cultivating a supportive relationship network involves nurturing connections with friends and family while harmoniously balancing the time and attention dedicated to these external relationships with that of the primary partnership. Let's explore the dynamics of building a supportive relationship network while maintaining equilibrium between external connections and the relationship.

Nurturing Relationships with Friends and Family:

Investing time and effort in nurturing relationships beyond the romantic partnership is crucial. Friends and family form a crucial support system, offering diverse perspectives, emotional support, and shared memories. Cultivating these connections strengthens the overall social fabric and contributes to individual well-being.

The Role of a Supportive Network in Relationship Success:

A robust support network acts as a pillar for relationship success. It provides a safety net during challenging times, offers advice and different viewpoints, and contributes to personal growth. A supportive network bolsters the primary relationship by providing external perspectives and fostering a sense of belonging.

Balancing Time and Attention:

Balancing time between the primary relationship and external connections requires thoughtful consideration. It involves allocating time and attention to nurture relationships with friends and family without compromising the quality and commitment to the primary partnership. Finding this equilibrium ensures that both areas receive the necessary nurturing without one overshadowing the other.

Strategies for Balance:

1. **Scheduled Time for External Connections:** Allocate dedicated time for interactions with friends and family. This allows for nurturing these connections without encroaching on quality time with your partner.

1. **Inclusive Activities**: Incorporate friends and family into shared activities with your partner. This fosters a sense of unity and enables everyone to connect, balancing external relationships within the context of the primary partnership.

1. **Communication and Planning:** Open communication about external connections helps in understanding each other's priorities. Planning events or gatherings in advance

allows for better time management and prevents conflicts between personal and partner time.

1. **Mutual Respect for Boundaries:** Establish mutual respect for boundaries. Both partners should understand and respect each other's need for external connections while maintaining a commitment to the primary relationship.

Valuing External Connections:

Recognize and celebrate the significance of external relationships. Friends and family provide a different kind of support and bring diverse experiences to enrich life outside the partnership. Valuing these connections contributes to personal growth and happiness, which positively impacts the primary relationship.

Prioritizing Quality Over Quantity:

The quality of interactions matters more than the quantity of time spent. Quality connections with friends and family add depth and fulfillment to life while maintaining a balance that ensures the primary relationship remains a priority.

Building a supportive relationship network involves nurturing connections with friends and family while maintaining a harmonious balance between external connections and the primary partnership. By nurturing these connections mindfully, valuing their role, and finding equilibrium in time allocation, individuals cultivate a robust support system that enriches life, contributes to personal growth, and complements the strength of the primary relationship.

AS WE CONCLUDE OUR exploration into the delicate balance of "Me-time or We-time," it becomes evident that navigating solitude and socializing is an art that requires intention, communication, and a commitment to understanding both personal and shared needs. In this chapter, we've delved into various aspects that contribute to a harmonious and fulfilling dating experience, recognizing the nuances that make each relationship unique.

Key Takeaways:

1. Value Alone Time:

- Recognize the importance of personal space and alone time as crucial components of self-discovery and rejuvenation.

2. Incorporate Healthy Alone Time:

- Strategies for integrating healthy alone time into relationships, ensuring that individuals have the space they need for personal growth.

3. Set Clear Boundaries:

- Communicate personal boundaries openly and honestly, creating a foundation of trust and respect within the relationship.

4. Navigate Social Anxiety:

- Tips for managing social anxiety in group settings, empowering individuals to engage comfortably in social events.

5. Cultivate Ease in Socializing:

- Strategies for cultivating a sense of ease during social events, making socializing an enjoyable and enriching experience.

6. Express Socializing Preferences:

- Explore how to communicate socializing preferences to find a balance that accommodates both introverted and extroverted tendencies.

7.Balance One-on-One Time:

- Recognize the impact of quality time on relationship satisfaction and the importance of balancing socializing with meaningful one-on-one moments.

8. Plan Inclusive Activities:

- Strategies for planning activities that cater to both introverted and extroverted preferences, fostering unity in diverse experiences.

9. Communication as the Key:

- Understand the pivotal role of communication in establishing balance, discussing personal needs, and creating a supportive environment.

10. Nurture External Connections:

- Recognize the value of nurturing relationships with friends and family, understanding the supportive role they play in relationship success.

11. Balance Relationship and External Connections:

- Strategies for balancing time between the primary relationship and external connections, ensuring a holistic and fulfilling life.

In finding the delicate equilibrium between solitude and socializing, couples embark on a journey of self-discovery, mutual understanding, and shared experiences. As we close this chapter, remember that the art of balance is an ongoing process—a dance that evolves with each step. May your "Me-time and We-time" be a symphony of harmony, creating a dating experience that is not only fulfilling but also resilient and enduring.

Conclusion

Chapter 8

"Pause for a moment, dear reader. What if this conclusion isn't an end but a reflective mirror, showcasing the transformative power of the strategies we've explored together?"

Recap of Key Strategies

PAUSE FOR A MOMENT, dear reader. This conclusion isn't merely an end but a reflective mirror, showcasing the transformative power of the strategies we've explored together. As we stand at the threshold of this enlightening chapter's closure, let's embark on a concise yet profound recap of the key strategies that have been the guiding stars in our pursuit of conquering dating anxiety and cultivating unshakeable dating confidence.

Chapter 1: Understanding Social Anxiety

In our initial exploration, we defined social anxiety in the context of dating, unraveling its roots and manifestations. We delved into the impact on self-perception, strategies for cultivating a positive self-image, breaking stigma, embracing vulnerability, and the profound mind-body connection.

Chapter 2: Choosing Comfortable Environments

Venturing into the realm of dating settings, we uncovered the importance of selecting environments that resonate with comfort. We discussed ideal date locations, the calming influence of nature, leveraging familiarity, personalizing experiences, and navigating public spaces with ease.

Chapter 3: Effective Online Dating Strategies

Transitioning into the digital landscape, we mastered the art of online dating. Crafting authentic profiles, mindful swiping, initiating conversations, moving from online to offline, and dealing with online rejection became essential skills in our toolkit.

Chapter 4: Mastering Conversation Skills

Words truly matter, and we explored the art of engaging conversation. Active listening, thoughtful questioning, sharing personal stories, navigating awkward silences, and building emotional intelligence became our compass for meaningful connections.

Chapter 5: Conquering the Fear of Rejection

Facing the formidable fear of rejection head-on, we cultivated a growth mindset, built resilience, set realistic expectations, and learned to move forward after rejection, emerging stronger and more resilient than ever.

Chapter 6: Creating Intimate Connections

Delving into the nuances of building deep connections, we emphasized the importance of emotional intimacy, gradual trust-building, recognizing and addressing trust issues, identifying shared values and goals, expressing affection authentically, and navigating vulnerability together.

Chapter 7: Balancing Alone Time and Socializing

Our journey culminated in exploring the delicate balance between solitude and socializing. Recognizing the value of alone time, strategies for incorporating it into relationships, effective communication about personal boundaries, managing social anxiety, and creating quality one-on-one time unfolded as key elements in our pursuit of dating harmony.

The journey has been transformative, filled with insights and strategies to navigate the complex terrain of dating with confidence. But this isn't the end—it's a point of reflection, a juncture to appreciate how far you've come and to propel yourself into the ongoing adventure of growth and self-discovery. Let's now shift our focus to highlighting the key takeaways from each chapter, distilling the essence of our exploration into actionable wisdom.

AS WE REVISIT THE CORRIDORS of our journey, it's essential to underscore the profound transformation from dating anxiety to dating confidence. Each chapter has been a stepping stone, a tool in your arsenal for navigating the intricate dance of relationships with newfound assurance.

Our exploration started with an understanding of social anxiety in dating, recognizing its roots and manifestations. We then transitioned into the importance of selecting comfortable environments, mastering online dating strategies, and honing conversation skills—equipping you with the skills to navigate the intricacies of modern dating.

In confronting the fear of rejection, we didn't just face it; we conquered it. We cultivated a growth mindset, embraced rejection as a catalyst for growth, and built resilience that fortified your spirit against the winds of disappointment.

Moving on, we delved into creating intimate connections—a realm where emotional intimacy, trust-building, shared values, and genuine expressions of affection became the building blocks for enduring relationships. Our journey concluded by striking a delicate balance between solitude and socializing, acknowledging the value of alone time and the significance of fostering meaningful one-on-one moments.

This journey has been more than a mere collection of strategies; it's a metamorphosis—a profound shift from the hesitations of dating anxiety to the confidence that emanates from within. Every insight gained, every challenge faced, and every triumph celebrated has sculpted a version of you that is resilient, confident, and ready to embrace the complexities of dating.

As we emphasize the transformative power of this journey, remember that confidence is not a static destination but a continuous evolution. You are now armed with the knowledge, resilience, and self-assurance needed to navigate the dynamic landscape of dating. The journey continues, and with each step, may your confidence blossom, guiding you towards the fulfilling connections you deserve.

Now, let's step boldly into the future, carrying the torch of confidence and self-discovery, ready to embrace the next chapters of your personal and relational growth.

Encouragement for Ongoing Growth

AS WE STAND AT THE intersection of reflection and anticipation, it's crucial to recognize that building dating confidence is not a destination but a continuous journey. The wisdom gleaned from this exploration is not the culmination but the foundation for ongoing growth—a perpetual process that transforms challenges into opportunities and moments of vulnerability into wellsprings of strength.

The journey we've embarked upon is a testament to your resilience, openness to change, and the commitment to personal growth. Remember, confidence isn't a fixed state; it evolves with every experience, every lesson learned, and every step taken outside your comfort zone.

Building Dating Confidence is Ongoing:

Let this be a gentle reminder that building dating confidence is not a one-time achievement. It's a dynamic process, an ever-unfolding narrative where each interaction, each connection, contributes to the canvas of your confidence. Embrace the notion that every date, whether filled with laughter or laced with challenges, is an opportunity to refine and reinforce the confidence you've cultivated.

Continue Applying Learned Strategies:

The strategies explored in this journey are not meant to be confined to the pages of this book. They are tools to be wielded in the real-world arena of dating. From choosing comfortable environments to navigating online dating with finesse, from mastering conversation skills to embracing vulnerability—let these strategies be your companions in the intricate dance of connection.

Seeking Personal Growth:

Beyond the realm of dating, this journey is a gateway to broader personal growth. The courage you summoned to face anxieties, the resilience you built to overcome rejections, and the vulnerability you embraced to forge connections—all contribute to your holistic growth. Keep seeking opportunities for self-discovery, understanding that a flourishing self is the foundation of meaningful relationships.

Embrace Your Unique Journey:

Each individual's path is unique, and so is your journey. There's no singular definition of success in dating confidence. Celebrate your victories, no matter how small, and be compassionate with yourself during moments of perceived setbacks. Growth is not a linear progression; it's a mosaic of experiences, each contributing to the masterpiece of your life.

Step Boldly into Your Future:

As you continue your journey, step boldly into the future, equipped with the resilience forged in the fires of challenges and the confidence that arises from knowing yourself deeply. Every date, every interaction, is an opportunity for growth, connection, and self-discovery.

May your journey be filled with enriching experiences, meaningful connections, and a deepening sense of self-assurance. Keep flourishing, keep growing, and may the chapters that follow be a testament to your continued evolution.

Sincerely,

Ember Blackwoods

Author's Note

Dear Readers,

As I pen down the final words of this journey, I'm filled with gratitude and anticipation. This book, a labor of love, is not just a collection of pages but a shared exploration of the intricacies of the heart and the triumphs over anxiety in the realm of dating.

Throughout these chapters, I've sought to weave together insights, strategies, and stories to accompany you on your quest for genuine connections. Dating can be a labyrinth of emotions, and I hope this book serves as a guiding light, providing comfort, understanding, and practical tools to navigate its twists and turns.

Remember, the pages ahead are not just words on paper; they are a conversation, an invitation to reflect, grow, and embrace the journey. Your resilience and courage inspire each sentence, and it's my sincere hope that you find both solace and empowerment within these pages.

Thank you for allowing me to be a part of your story. Here's to forging meaningful connections, embracing vulnerability, and finding the love that resonates authentically with your heart.

With warmth and anticipation,

Ember Blackwood

About the author

Ember Blackwood is a passionate new author dedicated to helping individuals find love and build meaningful connections. With a fresh perspective and a deep enthusiasm for the subject, Ember offers valuable insights and practical guidance to navigate the complexities of relationships.

As a new voice in the dating and relationship space, Ember brings a unique perspective and a genuine passion for helping others find happiness in their love lives. Through their writing, Ember explores various aspects of dating, including self-discovery, communication, online dating, and building healthy relationships.

Ember's engaging writing style captures the excitement and challenges of modern dating, making their books relatable and accessible to individuals at any stage of their dating journey. Their enthusiasm and dedication shine through, inspiring readers to embrace their authentic selves and approach dating with confidence and optimism.

Ember Blackwood's passion for helping individuals create fulfilling and authentic connections drives their work. As a new and enthusiastic voice in the field, Ember is excited to make a positive impact on the lives of those seeking love and companionship.

Also by Ember Blackwood

Dating

Comfort Zone Expansion: Introvert's Path to Dating Success
Dating with Confidence: Overcoming Pre-Date Anxiety
The First Date Playbook: Expert Tips for Memorable Dates
First Date Filter: Identify Red Flags, Preserve Your Time and Heart
Love in Full Bloom: Dating Secrets for Women Over 30

Standalone

The Geek's Guide to Love and Dating
Sis, Chill: Navigating Love with Confidence

About the Author

Ember Blackwood is a passionate new author dedicated to helping individuals find love and build meaningful connections. With a fresh perspective and a deep enthusiasm for the subject, Ember offers valuable insights and practical guidance to navigate the complexities of relationships.

As a new voice in the dating and relationship space, Ember brings a unique perspective and a genuine passion for helping others find happiness in their love lives. Through their writing, Ember explores various aspects of dating, including self-discovery, communication, online dating, and building healthy relationships.

Ember's engaging writing style captures the excitement and challenges of modern dating, making their books relatable and accessible to individuals at any stage of their dating journey. Their enthusiasm and dedication shine through, inspiring readers to embrace their authentic selves and approach dating with confidence and optimism.

Ember Blackwood's passion for helping individuals create fulfilling and authentic connections drives their work. As a new and enthusiastic voice in the field, Ember is excited to make a positive impact on the lives of those seeking love and companionship.

About the Publisher

About Ali the Narrator (Publisher)

Ali the Narrator is a fresh and enthusiastic publisher dedicated to helping authors navigate the exciting world of book publishing. With a deep appreciation for storytelling and a commitment to supporting authors, Ali the Narrator provides personalized and professional publishing services.

As a new publisher, Ali the Narrator brings a fresh perspective and a passion for discovering and sharing unique voices. They understand the challenges that authors face and are committed to providing guidance and support every step of the way.

With a focus on quality and attention to detail, Ali the Narrator offers a range of publishing services, including editing, formatting, cover design, and distribution. They work closely with authors to ensure that their vision is realized and that their books reach their intended audience.

Ali the Narrator takes pride in fostering a collaborative and transparent relationship with authors. They believe in open communication and strive to create a publishing experience that is both rewarding and enjoyable. With Ali the Narrator as your publishing partner, you can trust that your book will receive the care and attention it deserves.

Whether you're a first-time author or an experienced writer, Ali the Narrator is here to support you on your publishing journey. They are passionate about helping authors bring their stories to life and are excited to be a part of your publishing success.

Partner with Ali the Narrator, and together let's create a publishing experience that celebrates your unique voice and connects you with readers around the world.